Fundamental Testaments of the American Revolution

*Library of Congress
Symposia on the American Revolution*

Fundamental Testaments of the American Revolution

Papers presented at the second symposium, May 10 and 11, 1973

Library of Congress   Washington   1973

Library of Congress Cataloging in Publication Data

Library of Congress Symposia on the American Revolution,
   2d, 1973.
   Fundamental testaments of the American Revolution.

   Includes bibliographical references.
   1. Political science—History—United States—Congresses. 2. United States—History—Revolution—Congresses. I. United States. Library of Congress.
II. Title.
JA84.U5L5 1973   973.3'11   73-18173
ISBN 0-8444-0111-0

Advisory Committee
on the Library of Congress
American Revolution Bicentennial Program

John R. Alden
James B. Duke Professor of History, Duke University

Julian P. Boyd
Editor of The Papers of Thomas Jefferson, *Princeton University*

Lyman H. Butterfield
Editor of The Adams Papers, *Massachusetts Historical Society*

Jack P. Greene
Professor of History, The Johns Hopkins University

Merrill Jensen
Vilas Research Professor of History, University of Wisconsin

Cecelia M. Kenyon
Charles N. Clark Professor of Government, Smith College

Aubrey C. Land
Research Professor of History, University of Georgia

Edmund S. Morgan
Sterling Professor of History, Yale University

Richard B. Morris
Gouverneur Morris Professor of History, Emeritus, Columbia University

Preface

The papers published in this volume were delivered at the second Library of Congress Symposium on the American Revolution, held in the Library's Coolidge Auditorium on May 10 and 11, 1973. The first symposium, entitled The Development of a Revolutionary Mentality, was held at the Library on May 5 and 6, 1972. Additional symposia will be held each May through 1976. With the assistance of its advisory committee of distinguished historians, the Library has selected the following topics for future symposia in this series: leadership in the era of the American Revolution (1974); the impact of the American Revolution abroad (1975); and the incomplete Revolution (1976). The papers delivered at these symposia will also be published by the Library of Congress.

The Symposia on the American Revolution and the resulting publications are made possible through a grant from The Morris and Gwendolyn Cafritz Foundation, established by the late Mr. Cafritz, Washington realtor and philanthropist. Through this grant the Cafritz Foundation, which fosters cultural, educational, and developmental activities in the District of Columbia, has made a significant and lasting contribution to the understanding of the American Revolution.

The Library of Congress program to commemorate the Bicentennial of the American Revolution includes, among other activities, the preparation of guides to contemporary source materials in the Library, bibliographies on the Revolution, documentary and facsimile publications, musical programs, and exhibits. It also includes collecting copies of letters of Delegates to Congress, 1774–1789, for historical annotation and publication in a multivolume edition. Under the direction of the Assistant Librarian of Congress, the American Revolution Bicentennial Office in the Library has the responsibility for carrying out and coordinating these activities.

Elizabeth Hamer Kegan
Assistant Librarian of Congress

Contents

vii
Preface

3
Introduction
Julian P. Boyd

7
Common Sense
Bernard Bailyn

25
The Declaration of Independence
Cecelia M. Kenyon

49
The Articles of Confederation
Merrill Jensen

83
The Treaty of Paris of 1783
Richard B. Morris

109
The Fundamental Testaments Today
James Russell Wiggins

Fundamental Testaments of the American Revolution

JULIAN P. BOYD is editor of *The Papers of Thomas Jefferson,* president of the American Philosophical Society, Honorary Consultant in American History to the Library of Congress, and a member of the Librarian's Liaison Committee of Humanists and Social Scientists. He is a past president of the American Historical Association and has served on the National Historical Publications Commission, the National Portrait Gallery Commission, and the boards of trustees of the Institute for Advanced Study, the Henry Francis du Pont Museum in Winterthur, Del., and the Harry S. Truman Library Institute.

After receiving A.B. and A.M. degrees from Duke University in 1925 and 1926, Professor Boyd was a graduate student at the University of Pennsylvania and then, in 1928, was appointed editor of *The Susquehannah Company Papers* for the Wyoming Historical and Geological Society in Wilkes-Barre, Pa. He became director of the New York State Historical Association in 1932 and librarian and editor for the Historical Society of Pennsylvania in 1934. He accepted an appointment as Princeton University Librarian in 1940 and served in that capacity until 1952, when he joined Princeton's Department of History with the rank of professor, becoming emeritus in 1972.

Professor Boyd is currently at work on a complete revision of *The Declaration of Independence: Evolution of the Text* (1943, 1945), to be published jointly by the Library of Congress and the Princeton University Press. He was awarded the honorary degree of Doctor of Letters by Franklin and Marshall College in 1939, Duke University in 1951, Washington and Jefferson College in 1952, Rutgers University in 1956, Yale University in 1964, and Lehigh University in 1966. Bucknell University conferred the Doctor of Humane Letters in 1952.

Introduction

JULIAN P. BOYD

THE ERA OF THE FOUNDING FATHERS was to government what the age of Pericles was to art and the age of Elizabeth to exploration and discovery. In a favored land and on the foundation of ancient dreams, that remarkable generation dared to erect a new kind of society. Its unprecedented wager was that, under the governance of reason and the guiding principles of equality and justice, man's humane dispositions would triumph over his propensities for evil. This was a gamble of awesome proportions. Jefferson correctly described it as "an age of experiment in government" and the statesmen who were elevated to power and sustained by a politically astute people were very conscious, as historians are now discovering, that they were introducing a new era in human history.

John Adams thought we should celebrate the fateful decision of independence joyfully, with fireworks, bonfires, and the ringing of bells. So we have and so we should. But it is also fitting, particularly in this time of grave national crisis, that we should examine our beginnings in all humility, not in a spirit of reverence or uncritical adulation but to discover whether and how far the ship of state has been blown off its original course. From our somewhat perilous point of vantage, the greatest honor we can pay to that revolutionary generation is to inform ourselves, to try to understand, and to emulate if possible its courage in accepting the vast responsibilities consequent upon transference of sovereignty from a crown to a citizen. Their immense wager made this an inescapable obligation for every one of us.

Our national library—the greatest accumulation of recorded knowledge

Copyright 1973 by Julian P. Boyd

ever assembled and placed at the service of a people—has set the example for all other institutions of learning by basing its commemorative program upon Madison's fundamental proposition that liberty and learning are inseparable, each leaning upon the other for support. The series of symposia of which this is the second will bring together students, laymen, officials of government, and the public to hear what distinguished scholars have to say about various aspects of the American Revolutionary era. This is but one facet of the program that the Library of Congress has launched for the advancement of our knowledge about that epochal event. Its varied program, thoughtfully planned and ably administered, is designed to disseminate as well as to advance knowledge. This is in keeping with the Library's long tradition of service to the cause of learning and thus of liberty. Thomas Jefferson and James Madison, who planted the seeds of this great institution and who fully understood its indispensable role in the furtherance of self-government, would salute this as a worthy and dignified manner of commemorating their generation's aims and achievements.

But not everyone in their day—or, we must add, in ours—understood the essential need of such an institution in the conduct of free government. During the First Congress when a resolution was introduced to establish a Library of Congress, a writer in a Boston newspaper declared the proposition to be novel, absurd, and even unconstitutional. "Could anything be more foreign to the real business of congress?" he asked indignantly. "What connection has a library with the public? With our commerce? Or with any other national concern? . . . It is supposed that the Members of Congress are acquainted with history; the laws of nations; and possess such political information as is necessary for the management of the affairs of the government. If they are *not*," he concluded, "we have been unfortunate in our choice." Such observations made in the Age of Enlightenment—and coming from Boston, of all places—give pause to us who take our national library for granted much as we do the Rock of Gibraltar.

It has often been observed that, while the origins of other nations are lost in the dim mists of antiquity, our beginnings can be traced almost day by day in the resolves, petitions, and legislative records of committees of safety, colonial conventions, and the Continental Congress, on whose faithful secretary, Charles Thomson, was bestowed a privilege never before granted to any mortal—that of recording the birth pangs of a new nation. The papers presented at this second symposium will focus our attention on only four peaks of this vast Himalayan range of records in which the Declaration of Independence towers like Mount Everest above all others. There are many others which we might profitably discuss, as those who

Introduction

have planned these sessions well understand. There is, for example, the Virginia Statute for Religious Freedom, the counterpart in matters of conscience to the Declaration of Independence in its concept of government by consent. The Reverend Richard Price called it "an example of legislative wisdom and liberality never before known." He believed that if its principles had always been acted upon by civil governments, "the demon of persecution would never have existed: . . . truth and reason would have had fair play; and most of the evils which have disturbed the peace of the world and obstructed human improvement, would have been prevented."

There are many other noble peaks in this Himalayan range of testamentary acts and beliefs thrown up in the upheaval of revolution. George Mason's draft of the Virginia Declaration of Rights is one. Another is the Treaty Plan of 1776, enlarged and reinforced by that of 1784, by which the new nation sought to achieve commercial relations with the entire family of nations on the basis of open and equitable reciprocity. Another was the Treaty of Alliance with France, which made such strange bedfellows of absolutism and republicanism but which ensured the turning of the world upside down at Yorktown. Perhaps most creative of all, there are the Ordinances of 1784 and 1787 which rejected colonialism as incompatible with republican principles and which, contrary to what many thought to be the lessons of all philosophy and experience, enabled a new form of federal republic to be maintained over a vast extent of territory and indeed to expand itself westward across the continent and then, in our time, into the Arctic and the Pacific. The two great testaments that we will first consider epitomized the mind of Revolutionary America in a very special sense, the one in the area of public discussion and the other on the elevated plane of national purpose. Let us begin with Paine's *Common Sense,* which announced that the hour of decision was at hand and summoned the people's courage to make it.

Everyone knows what Theodore Roosevelt said about Paine, but who remembers John Adams' appraisal a century earlier? Call it, Adams wrote, dipping his pen in acid, "the Age of Folly, Vice, Frenzy, Fury, Brutality . . . or the Age of the burning brand from the bottomless Pitt . . . anything but the Age of Reason. I know not whether any Man in the World has had more influence on its inhabitants or affairs for the last thirty years than Tom Paine. There can be no severer Satyr on the Age. For such a Mongrel between Pigg and Puppy, begotten by a wild Boar on a Bitch Wolf, never before in any Age of the World was suffered by the Poltroonery of Mankind, to run through such a Career of Mischief. Call it then the Age of Paine." John Adams always said what he thought and usually what he thought makes us wish to know more.

To inform us of Paine's Common Sense, *no one is better qualified by long years of research and thoughtful reflection than Professor Bernard Bailyn. He is a native of Connecticut and a graduate of Williams College. He achieved his doctorate at Harvard, which never suffered him to depart and which in 1966 placed him in the distinguished chair of Winthrop Professor of History. Professor Bailyn began his scholarly investigations by studying New England merchants and shipping in the late 17th and early 18th centuries, a good background for his exploration and selective editing of the pamphlet literature of the Revolution. His first volume of* Pamphlets of the American Revolution *won the Faculty Prize of the Harvard University Press for 1965, and in 1968 his* Ideological Origins of the American Revolution *won both the Pulitzer and the Bancroft prizes. He will now illuminate for us Paine's* Common Sense, *a pamphlet which stirred the nation at a critical moment in world history.*

Common Sense

BERNARD BAILYN

Common Sense is the most brilliant pamphlet written during the American Revolution, and one of the most brilliant pamphlets ever written in the English language. How it could have been produced by the bankrupt Quaker corsetmaker, the sometime teacher, preacher, and grocer, and twice-dismissed excise officer who happened to catch Benjamin Franklin's attention in England and who arrived in America only 14 months before *Common Sense* was published is nothing one can explain without explaining genius itself. For it is a work of genius—slapdash as it is, rambling as it is, crude as it is. It "burst from the press," Benjamin Rush wrote, "with an effect which has rarely been produced by types and papers in any age or country." Its effect, Franklin said, was "prodigious." It touched some extraordinarily sensitive nerve in American political awareness in the confusing period in which it appeared.

It was written by an Englishman, not an American. Paine had only the barest acquaintance with American affairs when, with Rush's encouragement, he turned an invitation by Franklin to write a history of the Anglo-American controversy into the occasion for composing a passionate tract for American independence. Yet not only does *Common Sense* voice some of the deepest aspirations of the American people on the eve of the Revolution but it also evokes, with superb vigor and with perfect intonation, longings and aspirations that have remained part of American culture to this day.

What is one to make of this extraordinary document after 200 years? What questions, in the context of the current understanding of the causes and meaning of the Revolution, should one ask of it?

Copyright 1973 by Bernard Bailyn

Not, I think, the traditional one of whether *Common Sense* precipitated the movement for independence. To accomplish that was of course its ostensible purpose, and so powerful a blast, so piercing a cry so widely heard throughout the colonies—everyone who could read must have seen it in one form or another—could scarcely have failed to move some people some of the way. It undoubtedly caused some of the hesitant and vaguely conservative who had reached no decision to think once more about the future that might be opening up in America.

For it appeared at what was perhaps the perfect moment to have a maximum effect. It was published on January 10, 1776. Nine months before, the first skirmishes of the Revolutionary War had been fought, and seven months before, a bloody battle had taken place on Breed's Hill, across the bay from Boston, which was the headquarters of the British army in America, long since surrounded by provincial troops. Three months after that, in September 1775, a makeshift American army had invaded Canada and taken Montreal. In December its two divisions had joined to attack Quebec, and though that attack, on December 30–31, had failed miserably, the remnants of the American armies still surrounded the city when Paine wrote *Common Sense,* and Montreal was still in American hands.

That a war of some sort was in progress was obvious, but it was not obvious what the objective of the fighting was. There was disagreement in the Continental Congress as to what a military victory, if it came, should be used to achieve. A group of influential and articulate leaders, especially those from Massachusetts, were convinced that only independence from England could properly serve American needs, and Benjamin Franklin, recently returned from London, had reached the same conclusion and had found like-minded people in Philadelphia. But that was *not* the common opinion of the Congress, and it certainly was not the general view of the population at large. Not a single colony had instructed its delegates to work for independence, and not a single step had been taken by the Congress that was incompatible with the idea—which was still the prevailing view—that America's purpose was to force Parliament to acknowledge the liberties it claimed and to redress the grievances that had for so long and in so many different ways been explained to the world. All the most powerful unspoken assumptions of the time—indeed, common sense—ran counter to the notion of independence.

If it is an exaggeration, it is not much of an exaggeration to say that one had to be a fool or a fanatic in early January 1776 to advocate American independence. Militia troops may have been able to defend themselves at certain points and had achieved some limited goals, but the first extended military campaign was ending in a squalid defeat below the walls of Quebec. There was no evidence of an area of agreement among the 13 separate governments and among the hundreds of conflicting American interests that was broad enough and firm enough to support an effective common government. Everyone knew that England was the most powerful nation on earth, and if its navy had fallen into disrepair, it could be swiftly rebuilt. Anyone whose common sense outweighed his enthusiasm and imagination knew that a string of prosperous but weak communities along the Atlantic coast left uncontrolled and unprotected by England would quickly be pounced on by rival European powers whose ruling political notions and whose institutions of government were the opposite of what Americans had been struggling to preserve. The most obvious presumption of all was that the liberties Americans sought were British in their nature: they had been achieved by Britain over the centuries and had been embedded in a constitution whose wonderfully contrived balance between the needs of the state and the rights of the individual was thought throughout the western world to be one of the finest human achievements. It was obvious too, of course, that something had gone wrong recently. It was generally agreed in the colonies that the famous balance of the constitution, in Britain and America, had been thrown off by a vicious gang of ministers greedy for power, and that their attention had been drawn to the colonies by the misrepresentations of certain colonial officeholders who hoped to find an open route to influence and fortune in the enlargement of Crown power in the colonies. But the British constitution had been under attack before, and although at certain junctures in the past drastic action had been necessary to reestablish the balance, no one of any importance had ever concluded that the constitution itself was at fault; no one had ever cast doubt on the principle that liberty, as the colonists knew it, rested on —had in fact been created by—the stable balancing of the three essential socioconstitutional orders, the monarchy, the nobility, and the people at large, each with its appropriate organ of government: the Crown, the House of Lords, and the House of Commons. If the balance had momentarily been thrown off, let Americans, like Britishers in former ages, fight to restore it: force the evildoers out, and recover the protection of the only system ever known to guarantee both liberty and order. America had flourished under that benign system, and it was simply common sense to try to restore its balance. Why should one want to destroy the most successful political structure in the world, which had been constructed by generations of constitutional architects, each building on and refining the wisdom of his predecessors, simply because its present managers were vicious or criminal? And was it reasonable to think that these ill-coordinated, weak communities along the Atlantic coast could defeat England in war and then construct a system of government free of the defects that had been revealed in the almost-perfect English system?

Since we know how it came out, these seem rather artificial and rhetorical questions. But in early January 1776 they were vital and urgent, and *Common Sense* was written to answer them. There was open warfare between England and America, but though confidence in the English government had been severely eroded, the weight of opinion still favored restoration of the situation as it had been before 1764, a position arrived at not by argument so much as by recognition of the obvious sense of the matter, which was rooted in the deepest presuppositions of the time.

In the weeks when *Common Sense* was being written the future—even the very immediate future—was entirely obscure; the situation was malleable in the extreme. No one then could confidently say which course history would later declare to have been the right course to have followed. No one then could know who would later be seen to have been heroes and who weaklings or villains. No one then could know who would be the winners and who the losers.

But Paine was certain that he knew the answers to all these questions, and the immediate impact that *Common Sense* had was in large part simply the result of the pamphlet's ringing assertiveness, its shrill unwavering declaration that all the right was on the side of independence and all the wrong on the side of loyalty to Britain. History favored Paine, and so the pamphlet became prophetic. But in the strict context of the historical moment of its appearance, its assertiveness seemed to many to be more outrageous than prophetic, and rather ridiculous if not slightly insane.

All of this is part of the remarkable history of the pamphlet, part of the extraordinary impact it had upon contemporaries' awareness. Yet I do not think that, at this distance in time and in the context of what we now know about the causes of the Revolution, the question of its influence on the developing movement toward independence is the most useful question that can be asked. We know both too much and too little to determine the degree to which *Common Sense* precipitated the conclusion that Congress reached in early July. We can now depict in detail the stages by which Congress was led to vote for independence—who played what role and how the fundamental, difficult, and divisive problem was resolved. And the closer we look at the details of what happened in Congress in early 1776 the less important *Common Sense* appears to have been. It played a role in the background, no doubt; and many people, in Congress and out, had the memory of reading it as they accepted the final determination to move to independence. But, as John Adams noted, at least as many people were offended by the pamphlet as were persuaded by it—he himself later called it "a poor, ignorant, malicious, short-sighted, crapulous mass"—and we shall never know the proportions on either side with any precision.

What strikes one more forcefully now, at this distance in time, is something quite different from the question of the pamphlet's unmeasurable contribution to the movement toward independence. There is something extraordinary in this pamphlet—something bizarre, outsized, unique—quite aside from its strident appeal for independence, and that quality, which was recognized if not defined by contemporaries and which sets it off from the rest of the pamphlet literature of the Revolution, helps us understand, I believe, something essential in the Revolution as a whole. A more useful effort, it seems to me, than attempting to measure its influence on independence is to seek to isolate this special quality.

2

Certainly the language is remarkable. For its prose alone, *Common Sense* would be a notable document—unique among the pamphlets of the American Revolution. Its phraseology is deeply involving—at times clever, at times outrageous, frequently startling in imagery and penetration—and becomes more vivid as the pamphlet progresses.

In the first substantive part of the pamphlet, ostensibly an essay on the principles of government in general and of the English constitution in particular, the ideas are relatively abstract but the imagery is concrete: "Government, like dress, is the badge of lost innocence; the palaces of kings are built upon the ruins of the bowers of paradise." As for the "so much boasted constitution of England," it was "noble for the dark and slavish times in which it was erected"; but that was not really so remarkable, Paine said, for "when the world was overrun with tyranny, the least remove therefrom was a glorious rescue." In fact, Paine wrote, the English constitution is "imperfect, subject to convulsions, and incapable of producing what it seems to promise," all of which could be "easily demonstrated" to anyone who could shake himself loose from the fetters of prejudice. For "as a man who is attached to a prostitute is unfitted to choose or judge a wife, so any prepossession in favor of a rotten constitution of government will disable us from discerning a good one."

The imagery becomes arresting in part 2, on monarchy and hereditary succession, institutions which together, Paine wrote, formed "the most prosperous invention the devil ever set on foot for the promotion of idolatry." The heathens, who invented monarchy, at least had had the good sense to grant divinity only to their *dead* kings; "the Christian world hath improved on the plan by doing the same to their living ones. How impious is the title of sacred majesty applied to a worm, who in the midst of his splendor is crumbling into dust!" Hereditary right is ridiculed by nature herself, which so frequently gives "mankind an *ass for a lion*."

What of the true origins of the present-day monarchs, so exalted by myth and supposedly sanctified by antiquity? In all probability, Paine wrote, the founder of any of the modern royal lines was "nothing better than the principal ruffian of some restless gang, whose savage manners or preeminence of subtility obtained him the title of chief among the plunderers; and who, by increasing in power and extending his depredations, overawed the quiet and defenseless to purchase their safety by frequent contributions." The English monarchs? "No man in his senses can say that their claim under William the Conquerer is a very honorable one. A French bastard, landing with an armed banditti and establishing himself king of England against the consent of the natives, is in plain terms a very paltry rascally original." Why should one even bother to explain the folly of hereditary right? It is said to provide continuity and hence to preserve a nation from civil wars. That, Paine said, is "the most barefaced falsity ever imposed upon mankind." English history alone disproves it. There had been, Paine confidently declared, "no less than eight civil wars and nineteen rebellions" since the Conquest. The fact is that everywhere hereditary monarchy has "laid . . . the world in blood and ashes." "In England a king hath little more to do than to make war and give away places; which in plain terms is to impoverish the nation and set it together by the ears. A pretty business indeed for a man to be allowed eight hundred thousand sterling a year for, and worshipped into the bargain!" People who are fools enough to believe the claptrap about monarchy, Paine wrote, should be allowed to do so without interference: "let them promiscuously worship the Ass and the Lion, and welcome."

But it is in the third section, "Thoughts on the Present State of American Affairs," that Paine's language becomes most effective and vivid. The emotional level is extremely high throughout these pages and the lyric passages even then must have seemed prophetic:

Common Sense

The sun never shined on a cause of greater worth. . . . 'Tis not the concern of a day, a year, or an age; posterity are virtually involved in the contest, and will be more or less affected even to the end of time by the proceedings now. Now is the seed-time of continental union, faith, and honor. The least fracture now will be like a name engraved with the point of a pin on the tender rind of a young oak; the wound will enlarge with the tree, and posterity read it in full grown characters.

The arguments in this section, proving the necessity for American independence and the colonies' capacity to achieve it, are elaborately worked out, and they respond to all the objections to independence that Paine had heard. But through all of these pages of argumentation, the prophetic, lyric note of the opening paragraphs continues to be heard, and a sense of urgency keeps the tension high. "Everything that is right or reasonable," Paine writes, "pleads for separation. The blood of the slain, the weeping voice of nature cries, 'TIS TIME TO PART." *Now* is the time to act, he insists: "The present winter is worth an age if rightly employed, but if lost or neglected the whole continent will partake of the misfortune." The possibility of a peaceful conclusion to the controversy had vanished, "wherefore, since nothing but blows will do, for God's sake let us come to a final separation, and not leave the next generation to be cutting throats under the violated unmeaning names of parent and child." Not to act now would not eliminate the need for action, he wrote, but only postpone it to the next generation, which would clearly see that "a little more, a little farther, would have rendered this continent the glory of the earth." To talk of reconciliation "with those in whom our reason forbids us to have faith, and our affections, wounded through a thousand pores, instruct us to detest, is madness and folly." The earlier harmony was irrecoverable: "Can ye give to prostitution its former innocence? Neither can ye reconcile Britain and America. . . . As well can the lover forgive the ravisher of his mistress as the continent forgive the murders of Britain." And the sections ends with Paine's greatest peroration:

O ye that love mankind! Ye that dare to oppose not only the tyranny but the tyrant, stand forth! Every spot of the old world is overrun with oppression. Freedom hath been hunted round the globe. Asia and Africa have long expelled her. Europe regards her like a stranger, and England hath given her warning to depart. O! receive the fugitive, and prepare in time an asylum for mankind.

In the pamphlet literature of the American Revolution there is nothing comparable to this passage for sheer emotional intensity and lyric appeal. Its vividness must have leapt out of the pages to readers used to grayer, more stolid prose.

3

But language does not explain itself. It is a reflection of deeper elements—qualities of mind, styles of thought, a writer's personal culture. There is something unique in the intellectual idiom of the pamphlet.

Common Sense, it must be said, is lacking in close rigor of argumentation. Again and again Paine's logic can be seen to be grossly deficient. His impatience with following through with his arguments at certain points becomes almost amusing. In the fourth and final section, for example, which is on America's ability to achieve and maintain independence, Paine argues that one of America's great advantages is that, unlike the corrupt European powers, it is free of public debt, a burden that was well known to carry with it all sorts of disabling social and political miseries. But then Paine recognizes that mounting a full-scale war and maintaining independence would inevitably force America to create a national debt. He thereupon proceeds to argue, in order, the following: 1) that *such* a debt would be "a glorious memento of our virtue"; 2) that even if it *were* a misery, it would be a cheap price to pay for independence and a new, free constitution—though not, for reasons that are not made entirely clear, a cheap price to pay for simply getting rid of the ministry responsible for all the trouble and returning the situation to what it was in 1764: "such a thought is unworthy a man of honor, and is the true characteristic of a narrow heart and a peddling politician." Having reached that point, he goes the whole way around to make the third point, which is that "no nation ought to be without a debt," though he had started with the idea that the absence of one was an advantage. But this new notion attracts him, and he begins to grasp the idea, which the later federalists would clearly see, that "a national debt is a national bond"; but then, having vaguely approached that idea, he skitters off to the curious thought that a national debt could not be a grievance so long as no interest had to be paid on it; and that in turn leads him into claiming that America could produce a navy twice the size of England's for 1/20th of the English national debt.

As I say, close logic, in these specific arguments, contributes nothing to the force of *Common Sense*. But the intellectual style of the pamphlet is extraordinarily impressive nevertheless, because of a more fundamental characteristic than consistency or cogency. The great intellectual force of *Common Sense* lay not in its close argumentation on specific points but in its reversal of the presumptions that underlay the arguments, a reversal that forced thoughtful readers to consider, not so much a point here and a conclusion there, but a wholly new way of looking at the entire range of problems involved. For beneath all of the explicit arguments and conclusions against independence, there were underlying, unspoken, even unconceptualized presuppositions, attitudes, and habits of thought that made it extremely difficult for the colonists to break with England and find in the prospect of an independent future the security and freedom they sought. The special intellectual quality of *Common Sense,* which goes a long way toward explaining its impact on contemporary readers, derives from its reversal of these underlying presumptions and its shifting of the established perspectives to the point where the whole received paradigm within which the Anglo-American controversy had until then proceeded came into question.

No one set of ideas was more deeply embedded in the British and the British-American mind than the notion, whose genealogy could be traced back to Polybius, that liberty could survive in a world of innately ambitious and selfish if not brutal men only where a balance of the contending forces was so institutionalized that no one contestant could monopolize the power of the state and rule without effective opposition. In its application to the Anglo-American world this general belief further presumed that the three main socioconstitutional contestants for power—the monarchy, the nobility, and the people—had an equal right to share in the struggle for power: these were the constituent elements of the political world. And most fundamental of all in this basic set of constitutional notions was the unspoken belief, upon which everything else rested, that complexity in government was good in itself since it made all the rest of the system possible, and that, conversely, simplicity and uncomplicated efficiency in the structure of government were evil in that they led to a monopolization of power, which could only result in brutal state autocracy.

Paine challenged this whole basic constitutional paradigm, and although his conclusions were rejected in America—the American state and national governments are of course built on precisely the ideas he opposed—the bland, automatic assumption that all of this made sense could no longer, after the appearance of *Common Sense,* be said to exist, and respect for certain points was permanently destroyed.

The entire set of received ideas on government, Paine wrote, was false. Complexity was not a virtue in government, he said—all that complexity accomplished was to make it impossible to tell where the faults lay when a system fell into disarray. The opposite, he said, was in fact true: "the more simple anything is, the less liable it is to be disordered and the easier repaired when disordered." Simplicity was embedded in nature itself, and if the British constitution had reversed the natural order of things, it had done so only to serve the unnatural purposes of the nobility and the monarchy, neither of which had a right to share in the power of the state. The nobility was scarcely even worth considering; it was nothing but the dead remains of an ancient "aristocratical tyranny" that had managed to survive under the cover of encrusting mythologies. The monarchical branch was a more serious matter, and Paine devoted pages of the pamphlet to attacking its claim to a share in the constitution.

As the inheritor of some thuggish ancestor's victory in battle, the "royal brute of Great Britain," as he called George III, was no less a ridiculous constitutional figure than his continental equivalents. For though by his constitutional position he was required to know the affairs of his realm thoroughly and to participate in them actively, by virtue of his exalted social position, entirely removed from everyday life—"distinguished like some new species"—he was forever barred from doing just that. In fact the modern kings of England did nothing at all, Paine wrote, but wage war and hand out gifts to their followers, all the rest of the world's work being handled by the commons. Yet by virtue of the gifts the king had at his disposal, he corrupted the entire constitution, such as it was. The king's only competitor for power was the Commons, and this body he was able to buy off with the rewards of office and the intimidation of authority. The whole idea of balance in the British constitution was therefore a fraud, for "the *will* of the king is as much the *law* of the land in Britain as in France, with this difference, that instead of proceeding directly from his mouth, it is handed to the people under the formidable shape of an act of Parliament." Yet, was it not true that individuals were safer in England than in France? Yes, Paine said, they are, but not because of the supposed balance of the constitution: "the plain truth is that *it is wholly owing to the constitution of the people and not to the constitution of the government* that the crown is not as oppressive in England as in Turkey."

This was a very potent proposition, no matter how poorly the individual subarguments were presented, for it was well known that even in the best of times formal constitutional theory in England bore only a vague relation to the informal, ordinary operation of the government, and although penetrating minds like David Hume had attempted to reconceive the relationship so as to bring the two into somewhat closer accord, no one had tried to settle the matter by declaring that the whole notion of checks and balances in the English constitution was "farcical" and that two of the three components of the supposed balance had no rightful place in the constitutional forms at all. And no one—at least no one writing in

America—had made so straightforward and unqualified a case for the virtues of republican government.

This was Paine's most important challenge to the received wisdom of the day, but it was only the first of a series. In passage after passage in *Common Sense* Paine laid bare one after another of the presuppositions of the day which had disposed the colonists, consciously or unconsciously, to resist independence, and by exposing these inner biases and holding them up to scorn he forced people to think the unthinkable, to ponder the supposedly self-evident, and thus to take the first step in bringing about a radical change.

So the question of independence had always been thought of in filial terms: the colonies had once been children, dependent for their lives on the parent state, but now they had matured, and the question was whether or not they were strong enough to survive and prosper alone in a world of warring states. This whole notion was wrong, Paine declared. On this, as on so many other points, Americans had been misled by "ancient prejudices and . . . superstition." England's supposedly protective nurturance of the colonies had only been a form of selfish economic aggrandizement; she would have nurtured Turkey from exactly the same motivations. The fact is, Paine declared, that the colonies had never needed England's protection; they had indeed suffered from it. They would have flourished far more if England had ignored them, for their prosperity had always been based on a commerce in the necessities of life, and that commerce would have flourished, and would continue to flourish, so long as "eating is the custom of Europe." What in fact England's maternal nurture had given America was a burdensome share of the quarrels of European states with whom America, independent of England, could have lived in harmony. War was endemic in Europe because of the stupidities of monarchical rivalries, and England's involvements had meant that America too was dragged into quarrels in which it had no stake whatever. It was a ridiculous situation even in military terms, for neutrality, Paine wrote, is "a safer convoy than a man of war." The whole concept of England's maternal role was rubbish, he wrote, and rubbish, moreover, that had tragically limited America's capacity to see the wider world as it was and to understand the important role America had in fact played in it and could play even more in the future:

> . . . the phrase *parent* or *mother country* hath been jesuitically adopted by the king and his parasites with a low papistical design of gaining an unfair bias on the credulous weakness of our minds. Europe, and not England, is the parent country of America.

> This new world hath been the asylum for the persecuted lovers of civil and religious liberty from *every part* of Europe. . . . we claim brotherhood with every European Christian, and triumph in the generosity of the sentiment. . . . Not one third of the inhabitants even of this province [Pennsylvania] are of English descent. Wherefore I reprobate the phrase of parent or mother country applied to England only, as being false, selfish, narrow, and ungenerous.

The question, then, of whether America had developed sufficiently under England's maternal nurture to be able to live independent of the parent state was mistaken in its premise and needed no answer. What was needed was freedom from the confining imagery of parent and child which had crippled the colonists' ability to see themselves and the world as they truly were.

So too Paine attacked the fears of independence not defensively, by putting down the doubts that had been voiced, but aggressively, by reshaping the premises on which those doubts had rested. It had been said that if left to themselves the colonies would destroy themselves in civil strife. The opposite was true, Paine replied. The civil strife that America had known had flowed from the connection with England and was a necessary and inescapable part of the colonial relationship. Similarly, it had been pointed out that there was no common government in America, and doubts had been expressed that there ever could be one; so Paine sketched one, based on the existing Continental Congress, which he claimed was so fairly representative of the 13 colonies that anyone who stirred up trouble "would have joined Lucifer in his revolt." In his projected state, people would worship not some "hardened, sullen-tempered Pharaoh" like George III, but law itself and the national constitution, "for as in absolute governments the king is law, so in free countries the law *ought* to be KING." The question was not whether America could create a workable free constitution but how, in view of what had happened, it could afford not to.

So too it had been claimed that America was weak and could not survive in a war with a European power. Paine commented that only in America had nature created a perfect combination of limitless resources for naval construction and a vast coastal extension, with the result that America was not simply capable of self-defense at sea but was potentially the greatest naval power in the world—if it began to build its naval strength immediately, for in time the resources would diminish. So it was argued that America's population was too small to support an army: a grotesquely mistaken idea, Paine said. History proved that the larger the population the *smaller* and *weaker* the armies, for large populations bred prosperity and an excessive involvement in business affairs, both of which had destroyed the military power of nations in the past. The City of London, where England's commerce was centered, was the most cowardly community in the realm: "the rich are in general slaves to fear, and submit to courtly power with the trembling duplicity of a spaniel." In fact, he concluded, a nation's bravest deeds are always done in its youth. Not only was America now capable of sustaining a great military effort, but now was the *only* time it would *ever* be able to do so, for its commerce was sure to rise, its wealth to increase, and its anxiety for the safety of its property to become all-engrossing:

The vast variety of interests, occasioned by an increase of trade and population, would create confusion. Colony would be against colony. Each being able, would scorn each other's assistance: and while the proud and foolish gloried in their little distinctions, the wise would lament that the union had not been formed before.

So on the major questions Paine performed a task more basic than arguing points in favor of independence (though he did that too); he shifted the premises of the questions and forced thoughtful readers to come at them from different angles of vision and hence to open for scrutiny what had previously been considered to be the firm premises of the controversy.

4

Written in arresting prose—at times wild and fierce prose, at times lyrical and inspirational, but never flat and merely argumentative, and often deeply moving—and directed as a polemic not so much at the conclusions that opponents of independence had reached but at their premises, at their unspoken presumptions, and at their sense of what was obvious and what was not, *Common Sense* is a unique pamphlet in the literature of the Revolution. But none of this reaches its most important inner quality. There is something in the pamphlet that goes beyond both of these quite distinguishing characteristics, and while it is less susceptible to proof than the attributes I have already discussed, it is perhaps the most important element of all. It relates to the social aspects of the Revolution.

Much ink has been spilled over the question of the degree to which the American Revolution was a social revolution, and it seems to me that certain points have now been well established. The American Revolution was not the result of intolerable social or economic conditions. The colonies were prosperous communities whose economic condition, recovering from the dislocations of the Seven Years' War, improved during the years when the controversy with England rose in intensity. Nor was the Revolution deliberately undertaken to recast the social order, to destroy the last remnants of the *ancien régime*, such as they were in America. And there were no "dysfunctions" building up that shaped a peculiarly revolutionary frame of mind in the colonies. The Anglo-American political community could have continued to function "dysfunctionally" for ages untold if certain problems had not arisen which were handled clumsily by an insensitive ministry supported by a political population frozen in glacial complacency, and if those problems had not stirred up the intense ideological sensibilities of the American people. Yet in an indirect way there was a social component in the Revolutionary movement, but it is subtle and latent, wound in, at times quite obscurely, among other elements, and difficult to grasp in itself. It finds its most forceful expression in the dilated prose of Paine's *Common Sense.*

The dominant tone of *Common Sense* is that of rage. It was written by an enraged man—not someone who had reasoned doubts about the English constitution and the related establishment in America, but someone who hated them both and who wished to strike back at them in a savage response. The verbal surface of the pamphlet is heated, and it burned into the consciousness of contemporaries because below it was the flaming conviction, not simply that England was corrupt and that America should declare its independence, but that the whole of organized society and government was stupid and cruel and that it survived only because the atrocities it systematically imposed on humanity had been papered over with a veneer of mythology and superstition that numbed the mind and kept people from rising against the evils that oppressed them.

The aim of almost every other notable pamphlet of the Revolution—pamphlets written by substantial lawyers, ministers, merchants, and planters—was to probe difficult, urgent, and controversial questions and make appropriate recommendations. The aim of *Common Sense* was to tear the world apart—the world as it was known and as it was constituted. *Common Sense* has nothing of the close logic, scholarship, and rational tone of the best of the American pamphlets. Paine was an ignoramus, both in ideas and in the practice of politics, next to Adams, Wilson, Jefferson, or Madison. He could not discipline his thoughts; they were sucked off continuously from the sketchy outline he apparently had in mind when he began the pamphlet into the boiling vortex of his emotions. And he had none of the hard, quizzical, grainy quality of mind that led Madison to

Common Sense

probe the deepest questions of republicanism not as an ideal contrast to monarchical corruption but as an operating, practical, everyday process of government capable of containing within it the explosive forces of society. Paine's writing was not meant to probe unknown realities of a future way of life, or to convince, or to explain; it was meant to overwhelm and destroy. In this respect *Common Sense* bears comparison not with the writings of the other American pamphleteers but with those of Jonathan Swift. For Swift too had been a verbal killer in an age when pamphleteering was important to politics. But Swift's chief weapon had been a rapier as sharp as a razor and so pointed that it first entered its victim unfelt. Paine's writing has none of Swift's marvelously ironic subtlety, just as it has none of the American pamphleteers' learning and logic. Paine's language is violent, slashing, angry, indignant.

This inner voice of anger and indignation had been heard before in Georgian England, in quite special and peculiar forms. It is found in certain of the writings of the extreme leftwing libertarians; and it can be found too in the boiling denunciations of English corruption that flowed from the pens of such would-be prophets as Dr. John Brown, whose sulfuric *Estimate of the Manners and Principles of the Times* created such a sensation in 1757. But its most vivid expression is not verbal but graphic: the paintings and engravings of William Hogarth, whose awareness of the world had taken shape in the same squalor of London's and the provinces' demimonde in which Paine had lived and in which he had struggled so unsuccessfully. In Paine's pamphlet all of these strains and sets of attitudes combine: the extreme leftwing political views that had developed during the English Civil War period as revolutionary republicanism and radical democracy and that had survived, though only underground, through the Glorious Revolution and Walpole's complacent regime; the prophetic sectarian moralism that flowed from 17th-century Puritan roots and that had been kept alive not in the semiestablished nonconformism of Presbyterians and Independents but in the militancy of the radical Baptists and the uncompromising Quakers whom Paine had known so well; and finally, and most important, the indignation and rage of the semidispossessed, living at the margins of respectable society and hanging precariously over the abyss of debtors prison, threatened at every turn with an irrecoverable descent into the hell that Hogarth painted so brilliantly and so compulsively in his savage morality tales—those dramatic "progresses" that depict with fiendish, almost insane intensity the passages people in Paine's circumstances took from marginal prosperity, hope, and decency, through scenes of seduction, cruelty, passion, and greed, into madness, disease, and a squalor that became cosmic and apocalyptic in Hogarth's superb late engraving *The Bathos*.

These were English strains and English attitudes—just as *Common Sense* was an English pamphlet written on an American theme—and they were closer in spirit to the viciousness of the Parisian demimonde depicted in the salacious reportage of Restif de La Bretonne than to the Boston of the Adamses and the Philadelphia of Franklin. Yet for all the differences—which help explain why so many American radicals found *Common Sense* so outrageous and unacceptable—there are similarities too. In subdued form something of the same indignation and anger lurks around the edges and under the surface of the American Revolutionary movement. It is not the essential core of the Revolution, but it is an important part of it, and one of the most difficult aspects to depict. One catches a sense of it in John Adams' intense hatred of the Hutchinson-Oliver establishment in Boston, a hatred that any reader of Adams' diary can follow in innumerable blistering passages of that wonderful book, and that led to some of the main triggering events of the Revolution. It can be found too in the denunciations of English corruption that sprang so easily to the lips of the New England preachers, especially those most sunk in provincial remoteness and closest to the original fires of Puritanism which had once burned with equal intensity on both sides of the Atlantic. And it can be found in the resentment of otherwise secure and substantial Americans faced with the brutal arrogance and irrational authority of Crown officials appointed through the tortuous workings of a patronage system utterly remote from America and in no way reflective of the realities of American society.

Common Sense expresses all of this in a magnified form—a form that in its intensity no American could have devised. The pamphlet sparked into flame resentments that had smoldered within the American opposition to England for years, and brought into a single focus the lack of confidence in the whole European world that Americans had vaguely felt and the aspirations for a newer, freer, more open world, independent of England, which had not, until then, been freely expressed. *Common Sense* did not touch off the movement for a formal declaration of independence, and it did not create the Revolutionary leaders' determination to build a better world, more open to human aspirations, than had ever been known before. But it stimulated both; and it exposes in unnaturally vivid dilation the anger—born of resentment, frustration, hurt, and fear—that is an impelling force in every transforming revolution.

BERNARD BAILYN has been Winthrop Professor of History at Harvard University since 1966. He began his teaching career at Harvard in 1949, becoming an assistant professor in 1954, associate professor in 1958, and professor in 1961. From 1962 to 1970 he served as editor-in-chief of the John Harvard Library, and he is currently coeditor of the journal *Perspectives in American History*.

Professor Bailyn's publications include *The New England Merchants in the Seventeenth Century* (1955), *Massachusetts Shipping, 1697–1714* (1959), *Education in the Forming of American Society* (1960), and *Pamphlets of the American Revolution*, the first volume of which, published in 1965, was awarded the Faculty Prize of the Harvard University Press for that year. He is also the author of *The Ideological Origins of the American Revolution* (1967), for which he received the Pulitzer and Bancroft Prizes in 1968, and *The Origins of American Politics* (1968). He was coeditor of *The Intellectual Migration; Europe and America, 1930–1960* (1969) and of *Law in American History* (1972).

During World War II Professor Bailyn served in the Army Signal Corps and in the Army Security Agency. He received the A.B. degree from Williams College in 1945 and the A.M. (1947) and Ph.D. (1953) degrees from Harvard. He holds the L.H.D. from Lawrence University and Bard College and the Litt. D. from Williams College. He received the first Robert H. Lord Award of Emmanuel College in 1967.

Professor Bailyn is a member of the American Academy of Arts and Sciences, the American Philosophical Society, the Royal Historical Society, and the National Academy of Education and is a trustee of Manhattanville College.

And now we approach Mount Everest itself, the most elevated of all the majestic peaks in our Himalayan range of fundamental testaments. You will recall what John Adams said of this one also—that it contained nothing that had not been hackneyed in Congress for two years past. This missed the point, which Jefferson made clear. "Not to find out new principles, or new arguments never before thought of, not merely to say things which had never been said before," he wrote to Henry Lee in 1825, "but to place before mankind the common sense of the subject. . . . Neither aiming at originality of principle or sentiment, nor yet copied from any particular and previous writing, it was intended to be an expression of the American mind, and to give to that expression the proper tone and spirit called for by the occasion. All its authority rests, then, on the harmonizing sentiments of the day, whether expressed in conversation, in letters, printed essays, or in the elementary books of public right, as Aristotle, Cicero, Locke, Sidney, &c."

One of those essays he had himself written two years earlier, the famous Summary View of the Rights of British America. *Its authority rested there, but much of its power, of course, came from the felicitous language that Jefferson gave to the great document.*

The Declaration of Independence will be discussed by Cecelia Kenyon, Professor of Government at Smith College. She is a native of Georgia. She graduated from Oberlin, received her doctorate from Radcliffe, and has been teaching at Smith ever since. She is a distinguished and beloved teacher. Like Carl Becker, she has been sparing in her writing, but what she writes, also like Becker, has style, precision, and power. Indeed, in my opinion she is the first lady of American political theory.

"My heart belongs to the Revolutionary generation," she once wrote, "but I could not believe that the realism and authority of their thought could have sprung up merely from the pamphleteering of the 1760's. . . . It seems to me that the men of these [earlier] generations began to work out the theoretical problems English radicals of the 1640's only dimly perceived, and that John Locke either ignored or slurred over." Such probings of the origins of those concepts that were given expression in the Declaration of Independence have eminently qualified her to enlighten us about that most revolutionary of documents.

The Declaration of Independence

CECELIA M. KENYON

WHEN THE REPRESENTATIVES of the United States of America in General Congress Assembled adopted the Declaration of Independence on July 4, 1776, they accepted a theory of government with which they were generally familiar but the implications of which few of them had perceived or carefully explored.

> We hold these Truths to be self-evident, that all Men are created equal, that they are endowed by their Creator with certain unalienable Rights, that among these are Life, Liberty, and the Pursuit of Happiness—That to secure these Rights, Governments are instituted among Men, deriving their just Powers from the Consent of the Governed, that whenever any Form of Government becomes destructive of these Ends, it is the Right of the People to alter or to abolish it, and to institute new Government, laying its Foundation on such Principles, and organizing its Powers in such Form, as to them shall seem most likely to effect their Safety and Happiness.[1]

These concepts of natural equality, of natural rights and their preservation or security as the end of government, and of consent as the legitimate source of political authority had been widely disseminated throughout the colonies, and their expression in the Declaration of Independence could hardly have impressed most Americans as either alien or novel.

Yet a new force and authority were given to these familiar ideas by their embodiment in one of the fundamental testaments of the Revolution. The Declaration was an official state paper, and it came to be regarded as a symbolic expression of national identity. Its principles could not be formally abandoned or rejected without repudiating a national commitment. Furthermore, the inclusion of these concepts in the central theoretical

Copyright 1973 by Cecelia M. Kenyon

paragraph of the Declaration lent them additional status and prestige. Partly through structural organization and partly through elegant economy of style, Jefferson abstracted the principles of equality, natural rights, consent, and the right of revolution from other and sometimes competing contemporary values and gave first rank to the former by placing them among those truths held to be self-evident.

Some of the other and older concepts were expressed in the Declaration, while others were omitted. For example, the ideas that the public good was the purpose of government and the administration of justice one of its functions, appeared in the first and eighth counts in the indictment of George III. Other ideas were excluded altogether. There was no recognition in the Declaration of the traditional belief that the franchise should be restricted to men who demonstrated a permanent stake in society through the possession of property. There were references to God and to divine providence, but there was no indication of the widespread belief that government should attend to the moral virtue of its citizens and that one of the ways of doing so was to provide public support of religion and religious instruction. There was no specification of the proper structure or form of government—that was explicitly left to the discretion of the people—and thus no reflection of the belief that the rights of property should receive special protection by the institution of a second chamber of the legislature. Indeed, as we well know, the right to property was not listed in the Jeffersonian trilogy, though few Americans of the age would have denied that it belonged among those natural rights for whose security and protection governments were instituted. Therefore, although we should observe a seemly respect for Jefferson's statement, made late in his life, that he had intended the Declaration to be an "expression of the American mind," we must conclude that the expression he actually achieved was both limited and selective.

The theme of this paper will be the interplay of old and new ideas current in 18th-century America. I shall examine briefly the appearance of social contract theory and its alliance with the concepts of natural equality and rights in 17th-century English politics and ideology; I shall note the emergence of individualistic forces in the politics of middle and late colonial America, an emergence which antedated the widespread dissemination and acceptance of natural rights doctrine but which came eventually to blend with and reinforce that doctrine; finally, I shall examine one segment of the political thought of Thomas Jefferson, one of the few Americans to realize fully the individualistic and potentially divisive effects of the principles proclaimed in the Declaration of Independence, and to seek a theoretical redefinition of the public interest which would harmonize the new individualism with the older concepts of justice and the common good and which would therefore lend to republican government a stability which had hitherto been lacking.

The theory that government originated in a social or political contract has an ancient lineage in the history of Western political thought. It was familiar to the Greeks of classical Athens and was described in the first book of Plato's *Republic*. Its function there was to provide a foil against which Plato constructed his theory of justice, for the idea that government originated in contract was used to support the argument that conceptions of justice and of good and evil were derived from human convention, not from nature, and that therefore they were neither eternal nor universally valid. Thus, although one might derive a theory of anarchic individualism from this early version of contract doctrine, one cannot derive from it a justification of individual freedom and equality rooted in nature. It is customary for historians of political theory to trace the rudiments of modern contract theory to the coronation ceremonies of medieval monarchies. In these, the king traditionally took an oath to govern with justice, for the common good, and in accordance with the laws of God and of the realm. In return, the people through their symbolic representatives promised obedience and allegiance. The concepts of consent and of the common good as the end of government were undoubtedly present in these ceremonies, but there was no concept of the equality of the individuals who constituted "the people," or of their natural rights to individual liberty. Even the explicit contract theories of the late 16th century lacked any clear and unequivocal assertion of equality or of individual liberty. In the French Huguenot tract *Vindiciae Contra Tyrannos,* for example, the common good was still conceived of as a corporate entity which included, among other elements, preservation of the true religion. As late as 1637, Edmund Morgan has noted, John Winthrop of the Massachusetts Bay Colony used the compact theory of government to justify a restrictive immigration law, the object of which was to preserve social harmony and the true religion in that colony by maintaining ideological homogeneity among its inhabitants.[2] It was not until the doctrine of consent and contract was wedded to the doctrines of natural equality and natural rights that a philosophical basis for individualism was created.

This union had been effected by the time of the civil wars in England in the 1640's, and its results were clearly manifested in the arguments used to support demands for an extension of the suffrage and for reapportionment of representation in Parliament. The idea that man's original and natural freedom required his actual, individual, and continuing consent to government through exercise of the suffrage was expressed in Leveller manifestoes and pamphlets, and in the debates that took place among representatives of Oliver Cromwell's army at Putney in October of 1647.

The general subject of debate was the proposed Agreement of the People, a document intended to serve as a written, fundamental law for the government of England. One of the issues most sharply disputed was who constituted "the people," who, that is to say, would have the right to vote under the proposed new constitution. The radical position was stated by several officers and men, but by none more simply and eloquently than by Colonel Rainborough:

> I desired that those that had engaged in it[3] [might be included]. For really I think that the poorest he that is in England hath a life to live, as the greatest he; and therefore truly, sir, I think it's clear, that every man that is to live under a government ought first by his own consent to put himself under that government; and I do think that the poorest man in England is not at all bound in a strict sense to that government that he hath not had a voice to put himself under; and I am confident that, when I have heard the reasons against it, something will be said to answer those reasons, insomuch that I should doubt whether he was an Englishman or no, that should doubt of these things.[4]

Rainborough's appeal was to natural right, and it was immediately challenged by Henry Ireton:

> Now I wish we may all consider of what right you will challenge that all the people should have right to elections. Is it by the right of nature? If you will hold forth that as your ground, then I think you must deny all property too, and this is my reason. For thus: by that same right of nature (whatever it be) that you pretend, by which you can say, one man hath an equal right with another to the choosing of him that shall govern him—by the same right of nature, he hath the same right in any goods he sees—meat, drink, clothes—to take and use them for his sustenance. He hath a freedom to the land, the ground, to exercise it, till it; he hath the freedom to anything that any one doth account himself to have any propriety in.[5]

The clash between Rainborough and Ireton was a critical moment in the history of natural rights doctrine. Ireton saw, or thought he saw, the radical implications of the new principle of natural rights. If it were accepted, its ramifications could sweep away the institution of private property, and with it, the entire social, economic, and political structure of England. Before the new doctrine could be accepted and absorbed into the canon of English liberal politics, it had to be domesticated, its radical implications either withdrawn or obscured. It was the genius of John Locke to see the job that had to be done, and to do it with unobtrusive skill.

Locke accomplished the first part of his task in the famous chapter on the origin of private property. He reasoned that every man had a property in his own body and therefore in his own labor. Although the earth and its fruits were originally given to men in common, a man could legitimately appropriate something from that common stock of nature and make it his own by mixing his labor with it. In the early phases of the state of nature, before men discovered the use of money, men were forbidden to take from nature more than they could use; they were supposed to leave "enough" for the needs of other men; and they were forbidden to let anything taken from nature go to waste or be spoiled. As long as the original condition and its limitations prevailed, men's possessions remained roughly equal. But eventually men discovered the use of money. Money as a medium of exchange added to the convenience of trading, and for that reason, men consented to its use. Money did not spoil, and therefore men might accumulate considerable amounts of it without violating the prohibition against spoilage. Because some men were more industrious or wiser than other men, they accumulated more money than did those others. The use of money therefore resulted in inequality in the amount of property men possessed. Since men had consented to the use of money, they also consented to this result of inequality. The change in the distribution of property occurred while men were still in the state of nature. It was thus this property, unequally distributed, for the protection of which men entered into the social contract. The equality of condition characteristic of the early phases of the state of nature was therefore altered before men entered into civil society.

Thus Locke interpreted the natural right to property as a right to vested property and removed from the doctrine of natural rights the radical challenge to the security of property so feared by Henry Ireton in 1647. The conception of property in the *Second Treatise* was in perfect harmony with the status of property embodied in Magna Carta and deeply embedded in English law and tradition.

In his treatment of the principle of consent, Locke also tempered the radical equalitarianism expounded by the Levellers of 1647 and rejected by the more conservative opponents of Charles I. Locke reasoned that consent to a government could be given in two ways, expressly or tacitly. Since express consent was limited primarily to the original parties to the social or political contract, tacit consent was the form most commonly employed. Being tacit, it was ordinarily recognized by its signs, and of these, two were of primary significance. A son who inherited his father's landed estate—or any other form of property that could not be removed from the realm—gave his consent to government when he accepted his inheritance. By the acts of inheritance and tacit consent, he became a member of the society. Other men, not inheriting and not owning land or other immovable property, gave their consent to the government by remaining within its jurisdiction and accepting its protection. But they did not become members of the society. It would seem to follow, though Locke does not say so explicitly, that only the members of the society—those who owned landed estates or the equivalent—would be entitled to the franchise. Men without this kind of property lived in the society and consented to its government merely by not removing themselves elsewhere, but they did not vote. Thus, it would appear, Locke severed the connection between consent and the suffrage, and in a second significant way, removed, tempered, or obscured the radical implications which the doctrine of natural rights had had in the minds of both its advocates and its opponents a generation earlier.

Locke's achievement was therefore a dual one. By lending the weight of his reputation as a philosopher to the theory of natural rights and social contract, he gave that doctrine additional authority and perhaps facilitated its dissemination and popularization. By interpreting that doctrine in such a manner as to render it a reinforcement to the sanctity of vested property rather than an implicit threat, he transformed it into a doctrine with profoundly conservative implications for the social and economic structure of English institutions. Henceforth, the doctrine could serve as a kind of national platform to which Englishmen could subscribe as a useful instrument to combat and restrain absolute monarchy without opening the way to a radical reconstruction of their society.[6]

By the 1760's, when Americans began the protests against British parliamentary policies which eventually culminated in the decision for independence, the ideas associated with Locke's *Second Treatise* had been circulating in the colonies for half a century or more. The *Second Treatise* was not the only—and probably not the primary— means by which these concepts reached America, but the tendency of the colonists to take from English and European sources only those ideas which suited their purposes reduced the significance of variations among the different versions of natural law and contract theories. By the early decades of the 18th century, the colonies had developed a system and style of politics which, though modeled after that of the mother country, were nevertheless different in important respects. These differences affected the reception of what, for the sake of convenience, I shall call Lockeian ideas.

The two Lockeian concepts which met with the strongest resistance in colonial America were the idea of equality and the idea that the purpose of government was to secure the natural rights of men as individuals. Opposition to the first idea, equality, was expressed clearly and explicitly and is easily traced in the political sermons of New England clergymen. In 1722, William Burnham of Connecticut associated the idea of equality with "atheistical wits," argued that there could be no government at all if men's conditions were alike, and declared that God judged and determined what men's conditions in this world should be, "whether high or low . . . Rich or poore."[7] In 1740, William Cooper of Massachusetts preached: "The Notion of Levelism has as little Foundation in Nature as in Scripture."[8] Remarks of this sort were not unusual in the first half of the 18th century, nor were they peculiarly American. They gave voice to the venerable dogma of the Christian religion that held human inequality to be the result of divine providence. After the middle of the century, articulate expressions of this opinion tapered off, perhaps because the clergymen grew weary of fighting what they must by then have recognized to be a hopeless rearguard action, perhaps because resistance to the other Lockeian doctrine—the security of individual rights as the end of government—had also begun to soften though not to disintegrate.

It is more difficult to demonstrate colonial resistance to this second Lockeian concept, because the conflict between it and the concept which it partially displaced was indirect. The issue between the two concepts was rarely joined in the immediate and obvious manner in which Rainborough and Ireton had clashed over the concept of natural rights, or in the simple and overt fashion with which the New England clergy attacked the doctrine of levelism. It was rather an instance in which a people accepted a new ideology while still continuing to hold fast to an older concept with which the new doctrine was, if not totally incompatible, at least disharmonious. The older doctrine was based on the concept of the public good as a corporate entity, discoverable by men of good will through the use of their reason and, once discovered, having unquestioned priority over any individual or separate interests which might be in conflict with it. The new Lockeian theory did not abandon the concept of a public good, of course. But if its ramifications are closely analyzed, it would appear to require a new definition of that common good. If the purpose of government is to secure the natural rights of men as individuals to life, liberty, property, or the pursuit of happiness, what is common among these individual and potentially conflicting rights? Or how reconcile the now presumable priority of individual rights with the demands of the public interest? How, for that matter, can the public interest, the general welfare, the common good, now be either perceived or defined? I believe that the logical problems of natural rights doctrine were not fully recognized by Americans as they first came to accept and use that doctrine. Instead, they continued to believe in the older concept of a common good and to defend its priority over separate and conflicting individual or group interests.

I find evidence for this retention of the older idea in the fear and denunciation of faction repeatedly expressed during the last decades of the 17th century and throughout the entire period of the 18th century, and also in the ceremonial pleas for and pledges of unanimity in the public councils which appear in the first half of the latter century. In 1704, e.g., the governor of Massachusetts expressed his desire for "freedom and unanimity" in the proceedings of the legislature. In 1705, the governor of New Jersey hoped for "Unanimity in your Consultations." In 1717, another governor of Massachusetts again asked for "unanimity and a single aim at the Publick Good. . . ." In the next year, Lieutenant Governor Spotswood of Virginia said that he would continue "to oppose that restless faction which seems to be unhappily entailed upon this Government, and whose Machinations have in all Governours times disturbed the Publick Tranquillity of the Colony, merely to gratify their own private Resentments." In South Carolina a few years later, the council welcomed a new governor with this pious promise: "We know nothing can be more Disagreeable to your Excellency and Fatal to the well being of this Province, than keeping up Divisions, and therefore we assure You Sir, that we will do all in our power to Discountenance such practices. . . ." Such exhortations and pledges continued in the following decades. Even as late as 1763, in a speech celebrating the Treaty of Paris and the end of the French and Indian War, Governor Bernard advised the council of the Massachusetts legislature that "Unanimity, which I cannot too often recommend, was never more expedient than now. . . ."[9]

Laments about the prevalence of faction were also numerous. Samuel Willard warned against "Sinister Aims" in 1694; in 1710, Eliphalet Adams admonished the administrators of justice to guard against "private and particular interests." In 1717 Timothy Cutler exhorted his listeners not to choose men to "advance a particular interest, to Abet a Party, and Maintain a Faction."[10] Again, remarks of this nature were repeated for decades, but near the middle of the century their tone and even their content reveal a change. Factions continued to be deplored, but self-interest was no longer automatically denounced or attributed to evil motives. There were still occasional longings for unanimity expressed in the rhetoric of politicians on ceremonial occasion, but the rhetoric was rhetoric and no more.

I believe, then, that in the half century before the Declaration of Independence, the American people retained the old concept of a corporate public good as the end of government, and that their acceptance of the Lockeian ideology did not completely displace that older ideal. The latter kept alive and perhaps reinforced their fear of faction even as their society grew increasingly diverse and pluralistic, and as they continued to engage in the competitive politics which had characterized their behavior from the very beginning. But as the decades passed, they seemed to achieve a more realistic attitude toward the issues that divided them. Instead of perceiving disagreement in opinion and conflict of interest as unnatural and even sinful, they came to accept them as the normal though regrettable characteristics of republican—or quasi-republican—politics. This new attitude was succinctly expressed in a Massachusetts sermon delivered in 1765.

> Every large community is constituted of a number of little societies, in which there will be different branches of business. These, whatever pains are taken to prevent it, will have their different connections, and form separate interests; it is vastly difficult for those who govern, to keep the balance so exactly poiz'd that neither part may be injured; but much more, to prevent jealousies and suspicions that things are carried by favor and affection.[11]

Americans had at last come to recognize the inevitability, and therefore the limited legitimacy, of diverse and conflicting interests in society.

By 1776, this recognition had been strengthened by the nature of debate during the decade of colonial protest against British legislative policy. The aspect of that debate which is of particular relevance to the theme of this paper is the issue of representation. When Americans denied the authority of Parliament to levy taxes upon the colonists, on the ground that the latter were not represented in Parliament, British spokesmen responded with what came to be called the theory of "virtual" representation. The argument was that Members of Parliament represented the entire nation, indeed the entire empire, not merely the districts or electors who had actually sent them to the House of Commons. It was not necessary, the British asserted, that an individual or a group participate in an election in order for him or them to be authentically represented in Parliament. The majority of men resident in the home country either were not qualified to vote or lived in areas not yet granted a seat in the Commons, yet they were truly represented in Parliament. So likewise with the Americans; it did not matter that they did not vote in parliamentary elections. They were a part of the British nation and empire, and therefore they were "virtually" represented in the House of Commons.

Americans rejected this theory, and in doing so, called into question two of its major assumptions. They questioned the idea that the British people, nation, and empire had a single, unitary interest equally shared by all its members. They argued instead that the American colonies had interests that were separate from, and in conflict with, the interests of the British who lived in the British Isles. They also questioned the British effort to separate representation from the process of election and accountability. To the rhetorical questions posed by James Wilson, the American answer was an unqualified "no." Wrote Wilson:

> Can members, whom the Americans do not elect; with whom the Americans are not connected in interest; whom the Americans cannot remove; over whom the Americans have no influence—can such members be styled, with any propriety, the magistrates of the Americans?[12]

The ideas expressed by Wilson and others who attacked the British theory of virtual representation were not altogether new; they were implicit in what had been common practice throughout most of the colonial experience, though not always admitted in formal statements of political theory. The process of articulating the principles implicit in the practice resulted in a theory of representation significantly different from that of the British, and of lasting importance for the future of American politics. One result of the newly articulated theory was an increasingly realistic analysis of republican or representative government.

It was a fortunate prelude to the American experiment in republican government that the primary target of opposition during the decade of colonial protest was Parliament and not George III. If the colonists had blamed only the king for their troubles, they might have exhausted their polemical talents in endless repetition of already well-worn attacks on the institution of monarchy or on the personal misrule of the current monarch. Because they had also to argue against Parliament, they were compelled to seek out the causes of what they perceived to be unjust as well as unconstitutional legislation enacted by a body which was at least partially representative. They could not avoid facing squarely the existence of conflicts of interest not only between rulers and people but also between different segments of the people. They saw that much of the legislation which was injurious to their interests was not injurious to the interests of Parliament's immediate constituents. In the end, this conflict of interests led them to secede from the empire. Before that final decision was made, the nature of the debate over representation led its American participants to conceive of "the people" not as an abstract or corporate whole but as a collectivity of individuals and groups with both common and conflicting interests and opinions. The older idea of unquestioned subordination of separate interests to the larger public interest never completely faded away; Americans throughout the 18th century continued to deplore the existence of party and faction. But after the final break with Great Britain, they were too sophisticated and too realistic to write, as Thomas Paine did, that "Public good is not a term opposed to the good of individuals; on the contrary, it is the good of every individual collected. It is the good of all, because it is the good of everyone: for as the public body is every individual collected, so the public good is the collected good of those individuals."[13]

The recognition of the legitimacy of separate individual or group interests which was brought to fruition in the argument against "virtual" representation had a byproduct—perhaps an unintended one. It served to undermine residual elements of elitism in American political thought and practice. The logic of the patriot theory of representation was not inexorable, but it was persuasive. To be legitimate, it was argued, a representative assembly must actually reflect and be responsible to the people whom it represents. But if the people are not regarded as an undifferentiated mass composed of identical and interchangeable parts but instead as individuals and groups with different interests and different opinions, then how can a line be drawn to separate those segments of the public which require or deserve representation and those which do not? The ultimate logic of the argument was to reflect all significant interests, including those of men who had little or no tangible property. And who could represent these different segments better than a man who was himself a member of them? That this kind of logic did have an impact on the thinking of Americans is indicated by the concept of representation expressed during the debates over ratification of the federal Constitution. Thus Melancton Smith of New York:

> The idea that naturally suggests itself to our minds, when we speak of representatives, is, that they resemble those they represent. They should be a true picture of the people, possess a knowledge of their circumstances and their wants, sympathize in all their distresses, and be disposed to seek their true interests.[14]

During the Jacksonian period, the logic of identity of interest and status between electors and representatives produced an express preference for mediocrity in all three branches of the government. But that story is beyond the scope of this paper.

The evolution of colonial politics and the exigencies of the debate with Great Britain had thus led gradually to a recognition of diversity of interest and opinion, and to a partial, limited acceptance of the legitimacy of self-interest in politics. That was one strand in the American political mind of the Revolutionary period. But for every statement reflecting this acceptance of the legitimacy of self-interest, one can find a score or more which express the older view, equating interest with faction and denouncing both as inimical to the common good and, after independence was declared, to the stability of republican government. How then could such a people, so divided not only among themselves but within themselves, possibly succeed in the experiments to which they committed themselves in the spring and summer of 1776?

What was needed, some philosophical master of politics such as Plato might have said, was a theory which provided clear and precise criteria for distinguishing legitimate from illegitimate interests or which established a definite hierarchy of values by which every opinion and every interest could be measured and assigned its proper place in an ordered scheme of things.

The Declaration of Independence did not offer that kind of ordered, rigorously logical theory. "We hold these Truths to be self-evident, that all Men are created equal, that they are endowed by their Creator with certain unalienable Rights, that among these are Life, Liberty, and the Pursuit of Happiness—That to secure these Rights, Governments are instituted among Men. . . ."

It is difficult to break into the flow of Jefferson's graceful language and dissect the meaning and implications of the principles so eloquently expressed. But it is necessary to do so if we are to understand the radical nature of the theoretical basis upon which the Revolutionary generation initiated their experiments in republican government.

If one looks at the principles of government enunciated in the Declaration from the perspective of other theories of politics which have occupied a central place in the history of this subject, one is struck by the absence of a hierarchy of values and by the difficulty of giving precise definitions to the values that are said to be "self-evident." If one examines the Jeffersonian trilogy of rights, one cannot avoid the conclusion that only the first, and perhaps not even it, is susceptible to precise definition. Men of the 18th century probably had less difficulty than men of our own time in defining the nature of life and the right to it; to them, this right may have seemed self-evident not only in its existence but also in its definition or nature. But such a statement cannot be made concerning the second right in the trilogy, liberty. Jefferson's contemporaries knew or felt the difference between liberty and license, but the difference is of the category to be illustrated by example rather than defined with precision. Even if one succeeded in constructing such a definition, what assurance could there be that it would not become obsolete? Would not Jefferson be at least surprised and perhaps appalled at the appearance of a female scholar in the library of which his own treasured volumes formed the nucleus? The problems and ramifications multiply. If the liberty asserted by one man should come into conflict with the liberty asserted by another, how could the rights of both men be secured? What criterion could one devise to decide which assertion of natural right was the more valid?

Consider the third right in the trilogy: the pursuit of happiness. All of the problems pertaining to the right to liberty pertain with greater force to this right. Liberty was a word with a legal and constitutional history in the 18th century, and that history supplied some consensus as to its meaning. Happiness as an individual right was new, and it seems even more amenable to subjective interpretation than either liberty or life.

It is obvious, too, that the three rights can sometimes be in conflict with each other, and again there appears to be no criterion by which such conflicts can be resolved.

One cannot help but wish that the truths declared by Jefferson had been a little less self-evident to him and his contemporaries. One would not expect Jefferson to include within the Declaration a long disquisition on the various meanings of his terms and the multiple permutations involved in their possible relationships. But how tempting it is to wish that Jefferson had set himself the task of composing a substantial treatise in order to provide a systematic explication of the meaning of the Declaration of Independence. Jefferson shied away from systematic treatises on government, and with good reason.

Many of the problems that I have suggested could have been solved, at least partially and practically, had Americans followed the example of Thomas Hobbes and chosen absolute monarchy as their form of government. A monarch could have issued definitions by edict and resolved conflicts by fiat. The Americans chose representative republics instead. Whatever definitions were to be made would be made by the people; whatever compromises or conciliations of conflicting rights were to be effected would be effected by the people also. And, if I am correct in my analysis thus far, the people would have no fixed criteria to which they could resort for guidance in the resolution of disputes, and no authority apart from themselves upon whom they could rely for wise and just decisions. They were on their own.

The theoretical as well as the practical difficulty of the course upon which the men of the Revolution set this nation can be underlined by glancing briefly at other theories. Plato's model of a just society as presented in *The Republic* posited the existence of a universal and unchanging Good, knowledge of which was accessible to a select few. Knowledge of the Good entitled these few to rule absolutely and provided them with an objective and hierarchically ordered system of values to ensure that their rule was both wise and just. Their actual authority over the people was to be reinforced and exercised by indoctrinating the people with myths attributed to the gods, and when necessary, by the use of physical coercion. For many centuries, the dominant system of Christian political theory endowed the powers that be with the authority of God, commanded submission to these powers, presented authoritative guidance in the secular as well as the spiritual realm in the Word of God revealed in Scripture and through the Church, and reduced the likelihood of class conflict by the doctrine that inequality in the world of this earthly existence was the product of God's divine ordinance. Modern communism is not very different. In all its practical manifestations, it has a recognized canon of texts, a hierarchy of values, and authoritative interpreters of both canon and values; it has therefore a theoretical means for resolving conflicts of values and interests and for mobilizing the resources of the state for the achievement of prescribed goals.

In the beginning of the Republic, America had none of these theoretical aids to certainty, authority, and order. But the new nation was not without assets. It had, as I have emphasized, a long experience in a politics which, though not formally republican, did provide excellent and applicable preparation for that system. It also had, it may be said, a generation of men who were conscious of the problems and hazards of republican government, who regarded their own experiments as a laboratory for all mankind, and of whom some set their minds to the task of becoming good craftsmen in the design and operation of the new system. Of these men, it was the author of the Declaration of Independence who, more than any other man of the age, advanced toward a mature theory of republican society and politics.

Like most men of his generation, Jefferson had a sharp sense of the tenuous nature of the new experiments and of the fragility of the republican form of government. It is difficult for modern Americans to comprehend fully the grave and genuine doubts the men of the Revolution had that their experiments would issue in success. Because we are the heirs of their bold departure from the form of government which then had the best record for survival, we find it hard to believe that our Revolution, like the French, might have culminated in a military dictatorship, or that quarrels among and within the several states might have driven some of them back to the secure shelter of the British Empire. Such possibilities as these did not seem fantastic to sober men of 1776, 1787, or 1800. They knew that the surrender of General Lord Cornwallis at Yorktown did not ensure the achievement of their ultimate goals. It only meant that their experiments would, or could, continue.

Even as he was in Philadelphia preparing the Declaration of Independence, Jefferson began to direct his energy and intellect to the craftsmanship of long-range planning for republican government. In his thoughts on a new constitution for the state of Virginia, he made a tentative proposal which provides a key to a central theme in his design for a stable republic. He suggested that the standard property qualification for voting be ownership of 50 acres of land, but he also suggested that if a man did not possess 50 acres, the state should assign him that amount from the vast area of western territory to which Virginia then laid claim. Neither of these ideas was completely new. The idea of manhood suffrage had been proposed at least as early as the 1640's in England, and the comparatively easy availability of free or cheap land had characterized the American colonies from their earliest foundation. Yet I believe that Jefferson's linkage of the suffrage with a free gift of land did constitute a small revolution within the Revolution. For what he did was to turn inside out the traditional aristocratic notion that the right to vote should be restricted to those who had "a stake in society"—a stake usually represented by the ownership of land or some substantial urban substitute. The Virginia revolutionists did not embody Jefferson's proposal in their constitution of 1776, and Jefferson did not again press for its adoption in that precise form. But he never abandoned the underlying principle. It was at the very core of his political and social theory: if republican government was to endure, if the natural rights of man were to be realized, then every man must have a stake in that government which was the best means of securing those ideals. The stake had to be earthy, economic, materialistic, and it had to be substantial enough so that every man would recognize it as a stake and value it as such.

So central, constant, and pervasive was Jefferson's concern with property that it appears in his political thought, sometimes as an end, sometimes as a means, of good government. Consider, for a moment, the reflections on property and society occasioned by his experiences in France.

In October of 1785, Jefferson followed the French court to Fontainbleau for the annual hunting season. While he was there, he set out one morning to explore the countryside. His account follows:

I shaped my course towards the highest of the mountains in sight, to the top of which was about a league. As soon as I had got clear of the town I fell in with a poor woman walking at the same rate with myself and going the same course. Wishing to know the condition of the labouring poor I entered into conversation with her, which I began by enquiries for the path which would lead me into the mountain: and thence proceeded to enquiries into her vocation, condition and circumstance. She told me she was a day labourer, at 8. sous or 4 d. sterling the day; that she had two children to maintain, and to pay a rent of 30 livres for her house (which would consume the hire of 75 days), that often she could get no emploiment, and of course was without bread. As we had walked together near a mile and she had so far served me as a guide, I gave her, on parting 24 sous. She burst into tears of a gratitude which I could perceive was unfeigned, because she was unable to utter a word. She had probably never before received so great an aid.[15]

Two years later he went on a tour of southern France and northern Italy. Again he conducted an investigation into the living conditions of the poor, the method and purpose of which he reported to his friend the Marquis de Lafayette, to whom he also recommended a similar expedition.

This is perhaps the only moment of your life in which you can acquire that knolege. And to do it most effectually you must be absolutely incognito, you must ferret the people out of their hovels as I have done, look into their kettles, eat their bread, loll on their beds under pretence of resting yourself, but in fact to find if they are soft. You will feel a sublime pleasure in the course of this investigation, and a sublimer one hereafter when you shall be able to apply your knolege to the softening of their beds, or the throwing a morsel of meat into the kettle of vegetables.[16]

These observations of life in the French countryside served to reinforce Jefferson's convictions concerning the nature of the right to property and the just distribution thereof. As he wrote to the Reverend James Madison in the letter previously quoted, the existence of poverty and misery in a country where there was an abundance of uncultivated land indicated a serious infringement of man's natural right:

Whenever there is in any country, uncultivated lands and unemployed poor, it is clear that the laws of property have been so far extended as to violate natural right. The earth is given as a common stock for man to labour and live on. If, for the encouragement of industry we allow it to be appropriated, we must take care that other employment be furnished to those excluded from the appropriation. If we do not the fundamental right to labour the earth returns to the unemployed.[17]

If his observations of French rural life reinforced his conviction that every man had a natural right to property, or to the means of making a decent living as a substitute therefor, his observations of European cities, and especially Paris, fortified his belief that desperate poverty was incompatible with republican government. The reason was that conditions of poverty—extreme poverty—eroded man's moral sense, made it impossible for men to live honestly, tended to set each man against his neighbor. Jefferson's well-known hatred of cities and love of the countryside and of its yeomen farmers in America has sometimes been regarded as an archaic strand of 18th-century romanticism. Perhaps there was a touch of romanticism in his tendency to idealize the farmer. But his strictures on urban poverty and its effects on human personality do not today seem obsolete.

Shortly after he had received a copy of the Constitution of 1787, he wrote to his friend James Madison that, although he disagreed with some provisions of that document, he would willingly rely on the decision to be made on it by the American people. Why? His answer expressed his profound belief in the relationship between economic environment and political prudence and virtue:

This reliance [on the judgment of the people] cannot deceive us, as long as we remain virtuous; and I think we shall be that, as long as agriculture is our principal object, which will be the case while there remain vacant lands in any part of America. When we get piled upon one another in large cities, as in Europe, we shall become corrupt as in Europe, and go to eating one another as they do there.[18]

By 1805, when he had come to accept the necessity of some industrialization in the United States, he attempted to explain why, in 1782, he had so harshly criticized both industrialism and urbanism. "I had under my eye, when writing, the manufacturers of the great cities in the old countries, at the time present, with whom the want of food and clothing necessary to sustain life, has begotten a depravity of morals, a dependence and corruption, which renders them an undesirable accession to a country whose morals are sound."[19]

The direction of Jefferson's analysis is clear, and it never wavered. A free society rested ultimately on the virtue of its citizens, but that virtue did not operate in a vacuum. Nor was it some permanent, unalterable constant. It was strongly influenced, if not indeed conditioned, by its environment. The slumdweller of Paris and the yeoman farmer of Virginia might be equal in their potentiality for virtue, but that equality of potentiality was not, and ought not to be expected to become, an equivalence of performance and behavior.

It was not merely a matter of harsh slum conditions confronting their Parisian victims with a choice of either conscious virtue and starvation or conscious vice and survival. There was, or might be, an actual cognitive dissonance between the respective moral codes of the Virginia farmers and the Parisian poor. So far as I know, Jefferson did not discuss this cognitive gap in this particular context. He did discuss it, and with passion, with respect to the one people who were excluded from the comfortable pale of American economic security, the blacks.

In late 18th-century Virginia, blacks had a widespread reputation for being inferior to whites in morality as well as in intellect. Jefferson did not dispute the latter opinion, though he attempted to probe its validity, but he disagreed vehemently with the former notion. One of the pieces of evidence commonly cited to support the alleged deficiency in ethical behavior was the black slave's tendency to engage in theft, usually rather petty theft. Jefferson regarded the accusation as intellectually outrageous, the evidence completely unreliable, and the conclusion scientifically untenable. He gave his reasons:

> That disposition to theft with which they [Negroes] have been branded, must be ascribed to their situation, and not to any depravity of the moral sense. The man in whose favor no laws of property exist, probably feels himself less bound to respect those made in favor of others. When arguing for ourselves, we lay it down as a fundamental, that laws, to be just, must give a reciprocation of right; that, without this, they are mere arbitrary rules of conduct, founded in force, and not in conscience; and it is a problem which I give to the master to solve, whether the religious precepts against the violation of property were not framed for him as well as his slave? And whether the slave may not as justifiably take a little from one who has taken all from him, as he may slay one who would slay him? That a change in the relations in which a man is placed should change his ideas of moral right or wrong, is neither new, nor peculiar to the color of the blacks.[20]

The meaning, I think, is clear. The black slaves could not be expected to comply with the moral code of the white owner with respect to property, because that moral code did not provide for the slave any protection at all for his most fundamental and precious property, self-ownership in his own body, life, and labor. As Jefferson saw it, a moral code which excluded one portion of society from the benefits which its observance secured for other parts was, for that first part, not valid and probably not operable.

Such a code rested, therefore, not on consensus grounded in reciprocal and shared interests, but on force.

It is a bitter and tragic irony that slavery should have sharpened Jefferson's perceptions about the mutual relationships of morality, consensus, economic status, freedom, and republican government. In the past, republican governments had usually been of short duration because of internal dissension or licentious behavior. Jefferson's colonial predecessors, as we have observed, lamented the existence of factions and exhorted themselves and their peoples to seek unanimity in the public councils and to subordinate private or partial interests to the common good. They did not, I have suggested, fully accept the individualistic implications of natural rights doctrine, and there thus remained a tectonic fault in their theory of politics. Jefferson rewove the fabric of republican theory and eliminated that fault. He envisaged a wide distribution of landed property as a means of satisfying the basic material needs of men, and he proposed that the right to vote be extended so that it approached manhood suffrage. Every man would therefore have a solid economic stake in the society, and every man would possess the suffrage as a means of protecting that stake. The universal possession of such a stake, he believed, would tend to temper inclinations to the kind of rash or extremist actions that had destroyed republics in the past. It would not eliminate faction or factious conflicts, but it would lend to the fabric of republican politics an elasticity hitherto lacking.

A similar link between satisfaction of basic human needs and the possibility of a free society was adumbrated in Jefferson's brief remarks on the laws of property and the black slaves' attitude and behavior toward those laws. Voluntary obedience to laws derives partly from recognition of the legitimacy of the laws, and such recognition in turn depends on the belief that the laws do, by and large, provide protection for one's own interests and rights. If this recognition and belief are lacking, then fear or coercion will be necessary to compel obedience. To the extent that fear and coercion are thus used, the quality and degree of freedom enjoyed by a people are diminished. Therefore, it would seem, we are led back to Jefferson's insistence on satisfaction of the basic needs and interests of the population as a requisite condition of a government that can fulfill the purposes prescribed in the second paragraph of the Declaration of Independence.

Perhaps, too, we can see an empirical if not a logical connection between the right to liberty and the right to the pursuit of happiness. If the latter right is ignored or left for a long period of time unrealized, then a frustrated people may take action which will jeopardize the enjoyment of liberty. A society can remain free and maintain a stable republican government only when its laws and institutions embody and secure the basic interests of all the members of that society.

The problem would therefore appear to be how to ensure that the legal and political system of a society does indeed serve the needs and aspirations of the people. Jefferson's answer was twofold: first, create and maintain an economic system in which it is possible for every man to acquire the material needs of life without depriving his fellow men of the means of satisfying their similar needs; second, let such men, economically secure and possessed of a stake in the society, collectively make the ultimate decisions regarding leadership, law, values, and policy in that society. Rational self-interest and common honesty should then unite to ensure that in the long run, or on the average, the decisions of the people would be good ones, conducive to their own and the society's welfare.

The first of these situations, general economic security, is not easy to provide. Jefferson realized that it was the great good fortune of America to possess the means of economic security as a given condition—i.e., the existence of what appeared then to be an almost inexhaustible supply of arable land. This was the economic foundation of a free and republican society, and Jefferson was not embarrassed to link his treasured ideals of liberty to so earthy and materialistic a foundation. As he wrote to John Adams in 1813:

> Here every one may have land to labor for himself, if he chooses; or preferring the exercise of any other industry, may exact for it such compensation as not only to afford a comfortable subsistence, but wherewith to provide for a cessation from labor in old age. Every one, by his property, or by his satisfactory situation, is interested in the support of law and order. And such men may safely and advantageously reserve to themselves a wholesome control over their public affairs, and a degree of freedom, which, in the hands of the *canaille* of the cities of Europe, would be instantly perverted to the demolition and destruction of everything public and private.[21]

If Jefferson was optimistic about the prospects for liberty in America, it was because this country then had a vast reservoir of virgin land to serve as the primary economic foundation for republican government. The land still exists, but modern technology has vitiated the function Jefferson attributed to it. It no longer provides a natural basis for the wide distribution of economic wealth and independence Jefferson thought essential for the preservation of liberty. The implications of his theory are therefore somber. Unless a substitute for the original foundation can be discovered or created, the legacy of 1776 may be lost. Jefferson did not believe that the ideals of the Declaration of Independence could be realized by one generation, not even by the extraordinary generation to which he belonged. He shared the consciousness of his contemporaries that the Revolution and the political experiments associated with it would affect the lives of generations yet unborn. But he had perhaps a more sensitive awareness of the unfinished nature of the Revolution, and of the consequent necessity for each generation not merely to cherish and preserve the heritage of freedom but to enlarge and extend its promise to all the races of men.

Jefferson died on July 4, 1826, the 50th anniversary of the adoption of the Declaration of Independence. Ten days before his death, he wrote a letter—his last—in response to an invitation to celebrate the anniversary with his old friends and neighbors, the residents of Washington, D.C. He was already weak and ill, and thus unable to accept the invitation. His note was therefore one of momentary regret but of ultimate affirmation—affirmation and aspiration for the Declaration of Independence and its inner meaning:

> May it be to the world, what I believe it will be (to some parts sooner, to others later, but finally to all), the signal of arousing men to burst the chains under which monkish ignorance and superstition had persuaded them to bind themselves, and to assume the blessings and security of self-government. That form which we have substituted, restores the free right to the unbounded exercise of reason and freedom of opinion. All eyes are opened, or opening, to the rights of man. The general spread of the light of science has already laid open to every view the palpable truth, that the mass of mankind has not been born with saddles on their backs, nor a favored few booted and spurred, ready to ride them legitimately, by the grace of God. These are grounds of hope for others. For ourselves, let the annual return of this day forever refresh our recollections of these rights, and an undiminished devotion to them.[22]

Notes

[1] I shall use the Dunlap Broadside of the Declaration throughout this paper.

[2] Edmund S. Morgan, ed., *Puritan Political Ideas, 1558–1794* (Indianapolis: Bobbs-Merrill, 1965), pp. 143–44.

[3] That is, those who had engaged in the Agreement of the People and, by extension, all those who had opposed Charles I.

[4] Great Britain, Army, Council, *Puritanism and Liberty*, ed. A. S. P. Woodhouse (London: J. M. Dent, 1938), p. 53.

[5] Ibid., p. 58. I have in this case adhered to the original transcription, omitting later editorial additions.

[6] John Locke, *The Second Treatise of Civil Government*, in his *Two Treatises of Government*, ed. Peter Laslett (Cambridge: University Press, 1960), chapter 5, passim; chapter 8, sections 119-22.

[7] Connecticut Election Sermon, 1722, pp. 1-2, 5-6.

[8] Massachusetts Election Sermon, 1740, pp. 6-7.

[9] In sequence: *The Boston News-Letter*, October 23-30, 1704; Ibid., June 18-25, 1705; Ibid., May 27-June 3, 1717; Ibid., January 19-26, 1718; *The Boston Gazette*, December 25-January 1, 1721; *The Boston News-Letter*, May 26, 1763. (Dates cited are Old Style.)

[10] In sequence: Massachusetts Election Sermon, 1694, p. 27; Connecticut Election Sermon, 1710, p. 31; Connecticut Election Sermon, 1717, p. 43.

[11] Massachusetts Election Sermon, 1765, p. 14.

[12] James Wilson, *The Works of the Honourable James Wilson, L.L.D.*, ed. Bird Wilson, 3 vols. (Philadelphia: At the Lorenzo Press, printed for Bronson and Chauncey, 1804), 3:221.

[13] Thomas Paine, "Dissertations on Government," in *The Complete Writings of Thomas Paine*, ed. Philip S. Foner, 2 vols. (New York: Citadel Press, 1945), 2:372.

[14] Jonathan Elliot, ed., *The Debates in the Several State Conventions on the Adoption of the Federal Constitution* . . . , 2d ed., 5 vols. (Washington: Printed for the editor, 1836-45), 2:245.

[15] Thomas Jefferson, *The Papers of Thomas Jefferson*, ed. Julian P. Boyd (Princeton: Princeton University Press, 1950-), 8:681.

[16] Ibid., 11:285.

[17] Ibid., 8:682.

[18] This version of Jefferson's comment occurs in an enclosure sent with a letter to Uriah Forrest, December 31, 1787. Although Jefferson wrote to Forrest that the enclosure was a copy of remarks contained in a previous letter to James Madison, the actual text of the letter to Madison is somewhat different. For the letter to Madison, see Jefferson, *Papers*, 12:438-43; for the quotation from the Forrest enclosure, see Ibid., pp. 478-79. For Boyd's notes on the matter, see pp. 442-43 and 479.

[19] Thomas Jefferson, *The Writings of Thomas Jefferson*, Memorial Edition, Andrew A. Lipscomb, editor-in-chief, 20 vols. (Washington: Issued under the auspices of the Thomas Jefferson Memorial Association of the United States, 1903-04), 11:55.

[20] Ibid., 2:199.

[21] Ibid., 13:401-2.

[22] Thomas Jefferson, *The Life and Selected Writings of Thomas Jefferson*, ed. Adrienne Koch and William Peden (New York: Modern Library, 1944), pp. 729-30.

CECELIA M. KENYON, a native of Gainesville, Ga., received her education in the Gainesville public schools and at Oberlin College, Radcliffe College, and Harvard University. Dr. Kenyon has been a member of the faculty of Smith College since 1948 and Charles N. Clark Professor of Government at Smith since 1969. Her fields of teaching are the history of European political thought from Homer to Burke and of American political thought from the colonial era to the present.

A member of Phi Beta Kappa, the American Political Science Association, and the American Antiquarian Society, Professor Kenyon is at present serving on committees concerned with the celebration of the 200th anniversary of the American Revolution for the American Antiquarian Society, the American Historical Association, and the Library of Congress. She has presented papers at various professional meetings, is the editor of *The Antifederalists* (1965), and is the author of articles or reviews in the *American Political Science Review, William and Mary Quarterly, Harvard Law Review, New York Times* Book Section, *Encyclopaedia Britannica, Centennial Review, New York Review of Books, New England Quarterly,* and *Political Science Quarterly.*

Historians enhance our knowledge by the freedom with which they disagree and challenge each other and thus advance with their discoveries. This, in fact, is the first of their obligations. These symposia are organized on a rather old-fashioned concept, for there seems to be a tendency in some quarters today to get fresh viewpoints by asking those who know nothing of the subject to approach it from the outside. We, on the contrary, go to the authorities, on the assumption that information should preferably be obtained from those who know what they are talking about. To discuss the Articles of Confederation and the Treaty of Paris, we have the unquestioned authorities. Each of our speakers is preeminently and without question the authority—not just one of the leading authorities, but the authority *—on the document for which he speaks.*

"It is very doubtful," declared George Bernard Shaw in 1933, "whether man is enough of a political animal to produce a good, sensible, serious, and efficient constitution. All the evidence is against it." This observation of 1933, applauded in the way Americans seem to applaud criticisms coming from the land from which they declared their independence, only proved that a clever Irish playwright could be a very bad historian. An 18th-century European observer—I think he was a Frenchman—came closer to the truth when he said that Americans could make any *constitution work. So they could, and so they proved in the case of the first of our federal constitutions. That document, which has been seen by few except archivists and historians, is a beautifully engrossed parchment. It should stand midway between the Declaration of Independence and the Constitution in the hall at the National Archives. Metaphorically, that is where our next speaker has placed it.*

A native of Iowa, Professor Merrill Jensen is a graduate of the University of Washington, with his doctorate at the University of Wisconsin, where since 1964 he has been Vilas Research Professor of History. His Articles of Confederation, *published in 1940, established him at once as the authority on the origins and history of that document. He has been Harmsworth Professor of American History at Oxford and has given seminars in Japan in 1955, 1961, and 1964. He is a past president of the Organization of American Historians, and he is now crowning his career as editor of the documentary history of the ratification of the Constitution—the second most important of all the great series of documentary publications now in being. Since I am speaking in the presence of the editors of the Adams Papers, the Jay Papers, the Madison Papers, the Laurens Papers, the Letters of the Members of the Continental Congress, and other notable enterprises, I shall leave it to you to decide which is the first.*

The Articles of Confederation

MERRILL JENSEN

THE ARTICLES OF CONFEDERATION were a fundamental testament of the American Revolution because they were the first constitution of the United States. As a constitution the Articles were the product of Americans' experience with the British Empire, of their experience with one another, and of their reading of history and political philosophy.

But a common experience and a common education did not mean that Americans agreed when they wrote the Articles of Confederation any more than they agreed when they wrote the second constitution of the United States in 1787. Americans had different convictions about the nature and purpose of a central government, and they clung to their convictions with remarkable consistency throughout the Revolutionary era, although there were those who shifted from side to side for reasons ranging from sincere conversion to sheer political expediency.

Americans were divided by other than ideological convictions about government. The Articles of Confederation were also the product of social and economic differences and attempts to compromise them. What, for example, did southern planters and northern merchants have in common? Most of them would have answered, "Very little." Could a central government serve and protect their rival and often clashing interests? Many of them doubted it. Friendships and political alliances were formed across regional lines, but the same basic conflicts of interest that were debated in 1776 were debated again in 1787 and for decades thereafter.

It is not my purpose to present a technical analysis of the Articles of Confederation as a constitution but to place that document in the context of the history of the Revolutionary era and to set forth the issues of the

Copyright 1973 by Merrill Jensen

era as the men at the time saw them. They were men of surpassing skill at politics, sometimes on a deplorably low level, but at the same time they were men who could and did discuss government and society on the highest level. They differed in their vision of what the future of the new nation they created ought to be, and we have much to learn from their differences as well as from their agreements. We have not seen the likes of such men since then.

★ ★ ★

In the course of a century and a half as members of the British Empire, Americans laid claim to virtually all the rights and privileges and voiced most of the political and constitutional theories that they were to maintain in the debate with Britain during the decade before independence. They had in fact asserted the right to be taxed only by their own representatives and had denied the power of Parliament to legislate for them by the end of the 17th century.

In 1624, after the first legislature in America, the Virginia House of Burgesses, learned that the Crown would take over the colony, it enacted a law declaring that "the governor shall not lay any taxes or impositions upon the colony, their lands or commodities, other than by the authority of the General Assembly, to be levied and employed as the Assembly shall appoint."[1] Other legislatures made similar claims during the 17th century, and nothing essentially new was said about taxation thereafter.

By the end of the 17th century, too, some Americans had denied that the laws of Parliament applied to them. The Massachusetts General Court stated that position with utter clarity in 1677. The colony had refused to obey the Navigation Acts because, said the legislators, "we humbly conceive, according to the usual sayings of the learned in the law, that the laws of England are bounded within the four seas and do not reach America." The legislature had adopted the Navigation Acts as laws of Massachusetts because it had learned the king wanted them obeyed. Otherwise they could not have been enforced "without invading the liberties and properties of the subject. . . ."[2]

The assertion of such claims did not mean that Americans always achieved them or that they agreed with one another about those rights and privileges in practice. Americans shifted both arguments and sides depending upon the men or groups of men who stood to lose or to gain when they appealed to the central government for help or protection, or denied the right of that government to interfere.

The Articles of Confederation

What was new after 1763 was the attempt to establish in fact the control over the colonies which Britain had long held in theory. This involved, as never before, the intervention of Parliament, an intervention that meant limitation of the relative political and economic freedom to which Americans had grown accustomed. However, while Americans denied the right of Parliament to tax them, they did not agree about the role of a central legislature after 1763 any more than they did after 1776.

Thus in 1765, when the Stamp Act Congress proclaimed the right of Americans to tax themselves, it also declared that Americans owed "all due subordination" to "the Parliament of Great Britain."[3] The Congress lagged behind an important segment of public opinion. Shortly after it adjourned, the governor of Massachusetts reported that the "violent and foolish" among the Americans were asserting in their newspapers that the colonies were "perfect states, no otherwise dependent upon Great Britain than by having the same king; which, having complete legislatures within themselves, are no ways subject to that of Great Britain; which in such cases as it has heretofore exercised a legislative power over them has usurped it."[4] Parliament replied in the Declaratory Act that it had the power "in all cases whatsoever," and followed the declaration with such acts as the suspension of the New York Assembly and the alteration of the charter of Massachusetts.

American legislatures adopted forceful resolutions, and pamphleteers attacked each new encroachment, but they continued to lag behind popular opinion. It was not until the publication of Thomas Paine's *Common Sense* in January 1776 that a pamphleteer caught up with what newspapers such as the *Boston Gazette* and *New York Journal* had been saying for years, both in tone and argument. Thus in January 1773 the *Boston Gazette* stated flatly that "no people on earth have a right to make laws for the Americans but themselves," and if Britons continued their efforts to subject them, "we shall become a separate state."[5] In November, the *New York Journal* asserted that once the Crown had granted charters, "the persons to whom they were granted, and their associates, became a separate state, and were exempted from any obedience to any laws but those enacted by themselves or their legal representatives."[6] "Hampden" addressed "The Parliament of Virginia" and urged the House of Burgesses to change its name to Parliament. "The British Parliament," he said, "is nothing but your elder sister. Affection is due to her, but obedience is due only to the king," and if the king invades your rights, he ceases "to be king of the Dominion of Virginia."[7]

Before the end of 1773 the *Boston Gazette* bluntly proposed independence. It declared that Americans must unite to force their oppressors "to comply with the dictates of reason," and that "our politicians" had provided the answer to achieve that end: "Form an Independent state, an AMERICAN COMMONWEALTH."[8]

★ ★ ★

Americans united in 1774, but they did not create a commonwealth, nor did they declare independence. That they united at all was looked upon as something of a miracle. In 1760 an English traveler doubted that they ever could unite, "for fire and water are not more heterogeneous. . . ." He cited rivalries over trade and land and concluded: "In short, such is the difference of character, of manners, of religion, of interest, of the different colonies: that if they were left to themselves there would be civil war among them . . . while the Indians and Negroes would, with better reason, impatiently watch the opportunity of exterminating them all together."[9]

The first historian of the Revolution pointed to the same differences and concluded that the colonies united in 1774 only because they "were pressed by a common danger, threatening the most valuable rights of each individual province."[10] And more than 40 years after the Declaration of Independence John Adams agreed. He said that the union of the colonies in so short a time "was perhaps a singular example in the history of mankind. Thirteen clocks were made to strike together—a perfection of mechanism, which no artist had ever before effected."[11]

However exaggerated the differences among the colonies may seem to later generations, they were very real to the men of the Revolution. The social attitudes and economic interests of the "plantation colonies" were not the same as the "commercial colonies" of the North, and particularly those of New England.

Nothing, for example, is more evident throughout the Revolutionary era than the distrust and dislike of New Englanders. They had long had a reputation for dubious behavior as merchants and for religious bigotry. Among the many comments about New Englanders' commercial practices, none were more pungent than those in the New York newspapers after the breakdown of nonimportation in 1770. The Bostonians had been accused of cheating throughout, and when they attacked New Yorkers for abandoning their agreement, one New York newspaper replied that despite its glorious pretenses and resolves, Boston had been "the common sewer of America into which every beast that brought with it the unclean thing has disburthened itself."[12]

Nor did Americans in other colonies forget the hanging of Quakers in the 17th century. When the Massachusetts delegates stopped in New York on the road to the First Continental Congress, they met Philip Livingston. He talked of the "levelling spirit" of New England, mentioned the hanging of the Quakers, and apparently compared New Englanders to Goths and Vandals.[13] More than ancient history was involved, for New England Baptists appeared at the First Continental Congress to ask for relief from persecution by Massachusetts.[14]

New Englanders in turn looked upon people elsewhere as lesser folk lacking the virtues and advantages which New Englanders believed were theirs. John Adams summed up their attitudes better than most. He found very little good breeding in New York, did not see "one real gentleman," and complained that New Yorkers talked too loud and fast and never listened to answers to questions they asked.[15] After he had been in Philadelphia a month, he concluded that with all its trade and wealth, Philadelphia was not Boston. "The morals of our people are much better, their manners are more polite and agreeable—they are purer English. Our language is better, our persons are handsomer, our spirit is greater, our laws are wiser, our religion is superior, our education is better. We exceed them in everything, but in a market, and in charitable public foundations."[16]

As for southerners, after a long quarrel over army pay in which southerners insisted on greater differences in pay between officers and privates than New Englanders thought proper, Adams commented that "the characters of gentlemen in the four New England colonies, differ as much from those in the others, as that of the common people differs; that is, as much as distinct nations almost. Gentlemen, men of sense or any kind of education, in the other colonies, are much fewer in proportion than in New England." The southerners, because they were slaveowners and because their common people were very ignorant and poor, were "habituated to higher notions of themselves, and the distinction between them and the common people, than we are."[17]

New Englanders were canny politicians who did not let their convictions stand in the way of their goals. They were pleased that fiery southern orators in the first Congress made the New Englanders seem moderate men. And when Samuel Adams proposed that an Anglican clergyman open Congress with prayer, a Pennsylvanian told the Adamses that they "never were guilty of a more masterly stroke of policy."[18] An equally "masterly stroke" was John Adams' nomination of a Virginian in June 1775 to command the troops gathered around Boston. Although he thought it "whimsical," Adams knew that men in other colonies feared that New England would soon be full of veteran soldiers and in time "conceive designs unfavorable to the other colonies."[19]

General George Washington reacted to New Englanders like many another southerner. After he had been in Massachusetts a few weeks, he reported back to Virginia that "the people of this government have obtained a character which they by no means deserved; their officers, generally speaking, are the most indifferent kind of people I ever saw," and as for the men, "they are an exceeding dirty and nasty people. . . ."[20]

Such attitudes and opinions are but examples of the many differences among Americans that had to be managed and compromised to achieve independence and a central government, two issues so intertwined they cannot be disentangled.

★ ★ ★

The men who strove for independence showed little interest in the creation of a central government before 1776. The most consistent demand for such a government came instead from men who believed that independence would be followed by social and political upheaval. Some of them at first hoped to create an American government within the British Empire; later they argued that such a government must be created before independence; and after independence they continued to maintain that a government with power over the states and their citizens was indispensable. Their conviction was born of the realities of life in America as they saw them.

They predicted there would be civil war over boundaries and rival land claims, and they had reason for doing so. The quarrels among colonies over land became so intense after 1763 that by 1774 a civil war of sorts was under way between Pennsylvania and Connecticut settlers in the Wyoming Valley of Pennsylvania, and between Pennsylvania and Virginia over the headwaters of the Ohio River. And it seemed likely that the quarrel between New Yorkers and Vermonters would end in open warfare. In 1774 New York raised the reward for the capture of Ethan Allen to £100, and to judge from the attitude of New Yorkers, better dead than alive.

There were other portents of upheaval. After 1763 discontent led to the march of the Paxton Boys on Philadelphia, the tenant farmer rebellion in New York, and the Regulator movement in the Carolinas. In the course of these uprisings, Americans threatened to kill fellow Americans, and did kill them in North Carolina five years before the Declaration of Independence.

Most threatening of all, or so it seemed to some, was the rise of "new men," or "popular leaders" as they were commonly called, to real if not always legal power after 1763. They acquired power as ardent opponents of British policies and as equally ardent opponents of those members of the colonial political establishments who were reluctant to publicly join in opposition to Britain.

The popular leaders attracted a following among ordinary people by their arguments and their political methods. They attacked men in high positions as greedy officeseekers, as tools of British tyranny, and as rich men willing to sell the liberties of their country for money and political power. They mobilized hitherto inactive or passive segments of the populace and accustomed them to political activity as never before. Mass meetings put pressure on legislatures and individuals slow or reluctant to oppose British policies and adopted resolutions far more radical than most legislatures dared or cared to adopt. Furthermore, the mob, or the equally effective threat of mob action, was used to achieve ends which could not be achieved by legal means.

At the same time, the popular leaders proclaimed the right of the people to govern themselves, asserted that the sole end of government was the happiness of the people, and exalted the virtue and patriotism of the people in contrast to the iniquities of established leaders. Such proclamations were based on far more than the "rights of Englishmen" and the colonial charters; they were based on the "law of nature" and "natural rights," intangible foundations but no less heady for being so. As a New York newspaper proclaimed in 1768, "Vox Populi, Vox Dei, is the best political creed that was ever invented for a free people, and ought to be embraced by every lover of his country. . . ."[21]

The years before independence were indeed years when high principles were proclaimed in glowing rhetoric, but they were also years of ceaseless harassment of individuals, of beatings and tarring and feathering, of breaking windows and destroying houses, of burning boats and ships. And there was little or no protection from such assaults, for sheriffs and constables were powerless, and local militiamen were sometimes members of mobs or sympathized with them. Only the British army seemed to offer stability, as when the New York legislature unanimously called upon it to suppress the tenant farmer rebellion.

Thus, while the popular leaders were concerned with the threat of British tyranny and its American abettors, their opponents were far more concerned with the threat of the tyranny of the multitude; and the British connection, whatever the threat to American rights, seemed to them a lesser evil. They felt as Alexander Hamilton did when he told the Convention in 1787 that "the voice of the people has been said to be the voice of God; and, however generally this maxim is quoted and believed, it is not true in fact. The people are turbulent and changing; they seldom judge or determine right."[22]

The upheaval that accompanied independence was not as great as anticipated, but men's actions were shaped by what they believed would happen, not by knowledge of the future. And they were not silent. They denounced the popular leaders and their followers again and again, openly at first and then, as time went on, more discreetly but ever more fervently.

In an election sermon before the Massachusetts legislature in 1771, the Reverend John Tucker attacked "political zealots and pretended patriots" who were ready to "raise and promote popular tumults. . . . They cry up liberty, and make a mighty stir to save the sinking state, when in no danger, but from themselves, and others of a like cast."[23] Three years later John Randolph, attorney general of Virginia, addressed a pamphlet "to the public." "When I mention the public," he wrote, "I mean to include only the rational part of it. The ignorant vulgar are as unfit to judge of the modes, as they are unable to manage the reins of government." As for their leaders who claimed to be patriots, he declared, "I can by no means denominate a man a patriot because he enjoys the acclamations of the people."[24]

By 1774 some men were convinced that their only hope lay in reconciliation with Britain. Their views were stated with utter clarity by Gouverneur Morris in May 1774. For a decade, he wrote, the leaders of the people had "roared out liberty, and property, and religion, and a multitude of cant terms, which everyone thought he understood, and was egregiously mistaken." Now the port of Boston was closed and "the heads of the mobility grow dangerous to the gentry, and how to keep them down is the question." He said that what little remained of the spirit of the English constitution would give "the wealthy people a superiority this time," but they cannot keep all knowledge to themselves. "The mob begins to think and reason," and before long the "poor reptiles" will bite. The gentry fear this, but they will again deceive the people and that will mean "farewell aristocracy."

Morris' solution was "reunion with the parent state."[25] At the same time he drafted a plan for a central government. The idea was an old one, for Englishmen and Americans alike had been offering such plans ever since the end of the 17th century. It was not until 1754, however, that the Albany Plan went much beyond defense against the French and their Indian allies.[26] And the Plan was ignored or rejected by every American legislature to which it was submitted except that of New York.

Nevertheless, men continued to propose a central government which would, more effectively than Britain, check what they regarded as dangerous democratic tendencies in the colonies. In 1760 Dr. Samuel Johnson, president of King's College in New York, suggested the abolition of the charter governments because "in their present republican form, which is indeed pernicious to them, as their people are nearly rampant in their high notions of liberty," their rulers are afraid to do what is best and right. He suggested too that there should be an American legislature presided over by a "lord lieutenant." This legislature would "contribute to the union, stability, and good of the whole," consider common affairs of war and trade, and approve or veto the laws of each colony.[27]

Gouverneur Morris' plan in 1774 for "uniting the whole continent in one grand legislature" was in the same spirit. Morris was a realist, however, and he predicted that his plan would be opposed in America "since its tendency would be to give greater influence to the Crown, diminish the importance of each colony, and restrain the democratic spirit, which the constitutions and the local circumstances of the country had so long fostered in the minds of the people."[28]

Thomas Wharton, a Philadelphia merchant, who feared Pennsylvania backcountrymen rather than a city mob as Morris did, also wanted reconciliation and a central government. The government should have "power to make laws relative to the general police of America," a power which would have a "tendency of checking the turbulent spirit in any one of the colonies" and be a "proper check to the forward and ambitious views of any one colony." He reported early in July 1774 that it would be the intent of the forthcoming Congress "to endeavor to form a constitutional plan for the government of America. . . ."[29]

★ ★ ★

An American constitution was placed before the First Continental Congress, but the men who eventually shaped the outcome of the Congress had no "intent" of accepting that constitution or of letting the public know that it had been presented. The Congress was a remarkable assembly of leaders from 12 colonies, many of whom were to become conspicuous leaders of the new nation. Among them were the first two Presidents of the United States (illness kept the third President at home), the first Chief Justice of the United States Supreme Court, and many a future state governor and state and national officeholder.

The Congress divided almost evenly from the beginning, and the policies finally agreed upon were adopted by very narrow margins indeed. Thus when Richard Henry Lee proposed that American rights be founded on the law of nature, the colonial charters, the English constitution, and immemorial usage, he was supported by Samuel Adams, Patrick Henry, and Christopher Gadsden and was opposed by Joseph Galloway, James Duane, and John Rutledge, who were appalled by the "law of nature." John Adams, who had no more faith in the law of nature than its opponents, knew that ideas could be useful tools. He insisted upon it as "a resource to which we might be driven by Parliament much sooner than we were aware." The law of nature was agreed to, but only after weeks of wrangling.

Those who insisted upon using the law of nature also denied the authority of Parliament in all cases, including the right to regulate trade. James Duane and Joseph Galloway argued that Parliament did have the right, in fact had to have the right, or economic chaos would follow. In the course of the debate, James Duane referred, obviously with disapproval, to the Massachusetts act in 1677 which adopted the Navigation Acts as laws of the colony. Such men were defeated again, and on September 28, the day after Congress voted to recommend the nonimportation of British goods, Galloway and his supporters presented the outline of a constitution for an American central government within the British Empire.

Galloway told Congress that the colonies were totally independent of one another and that there must be a central government to regulate trade, paper money, and military forces and to settle the disputes between colonies over lands and boundaries. Either an American legislature had to be established with such authority or Congress should concede it to king and Parliament. Galloway's basic assumption was that "in every government, patriarchical, monarchical, aristocratical, or democratical, there must be a supreme legislature."

Congress debated Galloway's plan for a day and deferred consideration of it by a vote of six colonies to five. The plan was ignored thereafter, and when the journals of Congress were published, it was not in them.[30] Galloway then printed his constitution and his arguments for it in a pamphlet in which he declared that the only outcome of the Congress was "the ill-shapen, diminutive brat, INDEPENDENCY."[31]

Galloway raised a fundamental issue that Americans debated throughout the Revolutionary era and afterwards—the relationship between a central government and its legislature and the governments of the separate states. There was no break in the continuity of the debate, nor in the positions of many of the debaters. Richard Henry Lee and Patrick Henry, who opposed the Galloway plan in 1774, were conspicuous Antifederalist leaders 13 years later. Galloway was a Loyalist, but John Jay, John Rutledge, James Duane, and Edward Rutledge, who supported him in 1774, were Federalists in 1787. Jay was one of the authors of *The Federalist Papers,* which discussed the basic issues raised by Galloway and which came to many of the same conclusions. Furthermore, the men who wrote the second constitution of the United States consciously tried to reestablish the institutional means Britain had used to control the colonies—supremacy of a central legislature, appointment of state officials, veto of state laws, review of cases in a supreme court—and they hoped to succeed where Britain had failed. James Madison stated their purpose when he told the Convention in 1787 that the government it was creating would greatly reduce the powers of the states, and that "according to the views of every member, the general government will have powers far beyond those exercised by the British Parliament when the states were part of the British Empire."[32]

★ ★ ★

The men who shaped the final draft of the Articles of Confederation wanted no part of a government like that of Britain. The majorities in most American legislatures in 1776 and the men who elected them had no intention of surrendering any of the rights they had fought so long to achieve. Their views paralleled those of the colonial legislatures that rejected the Albany Plan in 1754. The Massachusetts General Court rejected it because "it would be subversive of the most valuable rights and liberties of the several colonies. . . ." Furthermore, it would have "great and extraordinary power" in time of peace as well as war, and "these powers are in the judgment of the two houses inconsistent with the fundamental rights of these colonies, and would be destructive of our happy constitution."[33] The Boston Town Meeting reinforced the argument by instructing its representatives in the legislature to oppose any plan of union "whereby they shall apprehend the liberties and privileges of the people are endangered."[34]

The Revolutionary leaders were men who believed in the sovereignty of the states, a belief stated concisely in 1775 by Samuel Adams, who declared that each legislature "is and ought to be the sovereign and uncontrollable power within its own limits and territories."[35]

The Virginia Convention stated the principle for Virginia and the other colonies as well when, on May 15, 1776, it instructed its delegates in Congress to move that Congress declare the colonies "free and independent states," and authorized them to agree to the formation of foreign alliances and a confederation. However, Virginia placed one restriction on what Congress might do, for it specified that "the power of forming government for, and the regulation of the internal concerns of each colony, be left to the respective colonial legislatures."[36] As the states wrote their constitutions, they made similar reservations in bills of rights.

Such declarations were in part the result of American experience with the central government of the empire and in part, of experience with the political elites of the colonies against whom the Revolutionary leaders had fought. English writings such as the letters of "Cato" and the *Political Disquisitions* of James Burgh confirmed their experience. These writings reiterated the proposition that the possession of power created a desire for ever more power by its possessors, and that the appetite for power must be checked or the liberties of the people would be endangered if not destroyed.

In the months before independence, Americans who demanded fundamental changes in the governments of the states-to-be wrote much about limiting the power of officeholders. They argued that Americans who held office in the new states would inevitably lust for power as British and colonial leaders alike had done in the past.

Among the testimonials to that conviction, none was more simply or eloquently stated than that of the people in the frontier town of Pittsfield, Mass. The Revolutionary leaders of the colony demonstrated that they did not want a revolution in Massachusetts, once they drove from office such men as Thomas Hutchinson and his allies, whom they had been calling "oppressors" and worse for more than a decade. In the summer of 1775 the Massachusetts Provincial Congress declared the Royal Charter of 1691 in effect, which meant that a hierarchy of appointed officials would continue to control local government.

The people in the west denounced the action and insisted on electing their own officials. In May 1776 the people of Pittsfield petitioned the legislature. They denied that the legislators had the power to impose a "fundamental constitution" because they were servants of the people and because "the people are the fountain of power. . . . That since the dissolution of the power of Great Britain over these colonies they have fallen into a state of nature."

The Articles of Confederation

The behavior of the justices of the peace appointed by the Revolutionary leaders led the Pittsfield petitioners to conclude that "every man by nature has the seeds of tyranny deeply implanted within him. . . ." "These," declared the petitioners, "are some of the truths we firmly believe and are countenanced in believing them by the most respectable political writers of the last and present century, especially by Mr. Burgh in his *Political Disquisitions,* for the publication of which one half of the Continental Congress were subscribers."[37]

Experience bolstered by theory helped shape revolutionary constitutions. Annual elections and rotation in office were adopted to thwart power seekers and would-be tyrants. The Pennsylvania constitution went the farthest in both practice and principle. Legislators could not serve more than four years in seven; councilors who served three years were ineligible for four, as were county sheriffs. And no Pennsylvanian could sit in Congress more than two years in any six. The purpose of rotation in office, declared the constitution, was to train men in public business, "and moreover the danger of establishing an inconvenient aristocracy will be effectually prevented."

The men who wrote the Articles of Confederation, without any argument whatever, provided that members of Congress must be annually elected, subject to recall at any time, and forbidden to serve in Congress more than three years in any six.

No one testified more clearly about the impact of such ideas than Alexander Hamilton in the first of his many essays urging the creation of a strong central government. Four months after the ratification of the Articles of Confederation, he wrote that "an extreme jealousy of power is the attendant on all popular revolutions, and has seldom been without its evils. It is to this source we are to trace many of the fatal mistakes, which have so deeply endangered the common cause; particularly that defect . . . A WANT OF POWER IN CONGRESS."[38]

★ ★ ★

The obstacles to the creation of a central government were great indeed, but Americans continued to debate the issue after the first Congress in 1774, which had assumed at least one function of a central government by adopting a policy of economic coercion that was enforced throughout America. The Second Continental Congress, which met a few weeks after the war began in April 1775, assumed major powers of a central government by creating a continental army, appointing generals to command it, and issuing paper money to pay for a war. The Congress had no legal or constitutional authority, yet in July, when Benjamin Franklin presented a constitution giving Congress those powers and others as well, his plan was relegated without debate to a pile of unfinished business.

The men who had supported the Galloway plan, and who later argued for the creation of an American government before declaring independence, opposed any attempt to consider a central government from the summer of 1775 to the spring of 1776. They did so because independence was the main issue in the second Congress, in fact although not in name, and they knew that the idea of a confederation was being used as a means of moving the colonies toward independence. Furthermore, the opponents of independence took positive action. In November 1775, John Dickinson, their leader in Congress, wrote instructions which were adopted by the Pennsylvania Assembly. The instructions ordered the Pennsylvania delegates in Congress to reject and dissent from any measure that might lead to independence "or a change in this form of government." New Jersey and Maryland soon sent similar instructions.[39]

Those instructions were evidence that some Americans were as afraid of a revolution in their governments as they were of Britain's evident intention to impose its will with military might. In June 1775, the New York Provincial Congress adopted a plan of reconciliation and instructed its delegates in Philadelphia to pay almost any price for it. "We must now repeat to you," stated the Congress, "the common and just observation that contests for liberty, fostered in their infancy by the virtuous and wise, become sources of power to wicked and designing men; from whence it follows, that such controversies as we are now engaged in frequently end in the demolition of those rights and privileges which they were instituted to defend."[40]

Privately, men expressed similar opinions throughout the winter of 1775-76. In April 1776, Carter Braxton, a Virginia delegate in Congress, said that if independence were declared, "the continent would be torn in pieces by intestine wars and convulsions."[41] Back in Virginia, his uncle, Landon Carter, was shocked by delegates in the Virginia Convention, who, he said, wanted independence so they could be "independent of the rich men" and be able to do as they pleased.[42]

John Adams, who worked as hard for independence as any man in America, recognized that troubles lay ahead. "All great changes," he wrote, "are irksome to the human mind, especially those which are attended with great dangers and uncertain effects." Americans might please themselves with the prospect of free and popular governments, but he predicted that in every legislature men would obtain influence "by noise not sense, by meanness not greatness, by ignorance not learning, by contracted hearts not large souls."[43] And he denounced demands for changes in the government of Massachusetts as "founded in narrow notions, sordid stinginess, and profound ignorance" and tending "directly to barbarism."[44] Yet Adams did not, like others who feared a revolution within America, look to a central government to prevent it. He had supported a confederation as a step to independence ever since July 1775, but not as an end in itself.

Congress remained deadlocked on the dual issues of independence and a confederation for months during the winter of 1775–76. But the deadlock was broken slowly by growing popular support for independence and by British measures which one by one destroyed the arguments and the hopes of men who wanted reconciliation. By May such men realized that independence was inescapable, and they changed tactics. John Dickinson, who had defeated an attempt to discuss a confederation in January, was by May the leader of those who demanded the creation of a central government before declaring independence.

John Adams was delighted with Dickinson's conversion. He reported on May 20: "Every post and every day rolls in upon us. Independence like a torrent." "What," he asked, "do you think must be my reflections when I see the Farmer himself now confessing the falsehood of all his prophecies, and the truth of mine, and confessing himself, now for instituting governments, forming a Continental Constitution, making alliances with foreigners, opening ports and all that. . . ."[45]

★ ★ ★

On June 7, 1776, Richard Henry Lee moved "all that" and John Adams seconded the motion. Lee's motion called upon Congress to declare independence, make plans for foreign alliances, and prepare a "plan of confederation." On June 12, two days after the vote for independence was put off for three weeks, Congress elected a committee of 13 to draft articles of confederation. The majority of those elected were opponents of independence or had argued for delay, including John Dickinson, Robert R. Livingston, and Edward Rutledge. The only open advocates of independence were Samuel Adams and Roger Sherman.

John Adams had pointed out that Americans had a choice: they could "declare the colonies a sovereign state, or a number of confederated sovereign states. . . ."[46] The committee chose to create a "sovereign state," and

John Dickinson undertook the task of drafting a constitution. On July 1, in his last speech against independence, one argument Dickinson used was that "the committee on confederation dispute almost every article. Some of us totally despair of any reasonable terms of confederation."[47]

The only member of the committee who left a record of his opinions was Edward Rutledge of South Carolina. He had supported the Galloway plan in 1774, but he opposed Dickinson's plan. He said it "has the vice of all his productions to a considerable degree; I mean the vice of refining too much." If it were not greatly curtailed it would not be adopted, and if it were adopted as written, "nothing less than ruin to some colonies will be the consequence of it." Rutledge declared that "the idea of destroying all provincial distinctions and making everything of the most minute kind bend to what they call the good of the whole, is in other terms to say that these colonies must be subject to the government of the eastern provinces."

Like many other southerners, Rutledge detested New Englanders. "The force of their arms," he said, " I hold exceeding cheap, but I confess I dread their overruling influence in council. I dread their low cunning, and those levelling principles which men without character and without fortune in general possess, which are so captivating to the lower class of mankind, and which will occasion such a fluctuation of property as to introduce the greatest disorder." Congress should therefore have no more power than absolutely necessary.[48]

Samuel Adams left no record, but he would have agreed with Rutledge that a central government should not be allowed to interfere within the states, a position he maintained throughout his political career. He might have remembered that one reason the Massachusetts legislature rejected the Albany Plan in 1754 was the concern over "the great sway which the Southern colonies . . . would have in all the determinations of the Grand Council."[49] Even if he did not remember, he probably shared the conviction of other New Englanders that the South would try to dominate the central government. A few years later William Gordon put that conviction succinctly when he wrote:

If America becomes an Empire, the seat of government will be to the southward, and the northern states be insignificant provinces. Empire will suit the southern gentry; they are habituated to despotism by being the sovereigns of slaves, and it is only accident and interest that has made the body of them the temporary sons of liberty.

The New Englanders should be resolute in retaining the sovereignty of the several states, and should look out in time against all distant encroachments.[50]

The Articles of Confederation

John Dickinson refused to vote for independence, and he left Congress before the constitution he had written was submitted on July 12. It was a subtle document that gave wide powers to Congress and guaranteed little to the states. For example, the draft provided that each state should "retain and enjoy as much of its present laws, rights, and customs, as it may think fit, and reserves to itself the sole and exclusive regulation and government of its internal police," but the guarantee was followed by a provision which negated its effect. The states were to retain those powers "in all matters that shall not interfere with the articles of this confederation." A similar guarantee accompanied by a similar reservation concerned the regulation of trade. The states could levy duties on imports and exports, but such duties could not "interfere with any stipulations in treaties hereafter entered into" with any foreign prince or state. Thus, while Congress was not given the specific power to regulate trade, it could do so by the use of its exclusive treaty-making power. Throughout the Dickinson draft there were other restrictions on the powers of the states. The sole restriction on Congress, and it was an important one, was that it could not levy taxes except to maintain a post office.

Congress contained lawyers as canny as John Dickinson, but at first they did not focus on the fundamental nature of his draft. They turned instead to provisions which pitted large states against small states, southern states against northern states, and states with charter claims to the "South Seas" against states with definite boundaries.

The Dickinson draft provided that each state should have one vote. The delegates from the three largest states—Virginia, with 20 percent of the population, and Massachusetts and Pennsylvania—argued that the states should vote according to their populations. The issue was not new. Seventy-five years earlier a Virginian had written a pamphlet attacking William Penn's proposed government because Penn assigned only two delegates to each colony and, what is more, located the capital in New York.[51]

The Virginians opened the debate in the first Congress in 1774 when Patrick Henry declared that all government was dissolved, that the colonies were in a state of nature, and that "the distinctions between Virginians, Pennsylvanians, New Yorkers, and New Englanders are no more." He concluded grandly, "I am not a Virginian, but an American." Some latter-day commentators have seen in Henry's rhetoric the spirit of nationalism. It was nothing of the kind. He was simply arguing that Virginia should have more votes than the small colonies, and his colleague Benjamin Harrison predicted that if Virginia did not get more votes, it would not attend another Congress. John Sullivan countered for the small colonies that "a little colony had its all at stake as well as a great one."[52] There were more small colonies than large ones, and they established the rule that each colony would have one vote.

When the debate resumed in July 1776, the Pennsylvanians took the lead. James Wilson, Benjamin Rush, and Benjamin Franklin used various arguments. Franklin predicted that any union based on the iniquitous principle of equality would not last long, and if the small states wanted equality, they should pay equal amounts of money. Benjamin Rush appealed to history to "prove" that the principle of equal votes was wrong, and, echoing Patrick Henry in 1774, declared that he was "not pleading the cause of Pennsylvania. When I entered that door, I considered myself a citizen of America." Franklin appealed to more recent history. The objections of the small states, he said, were the same as those made against the union between England and Scotland, and the predictions had been wrong. Dr. John Witherspoon, president of the College of New Jersey and a Scot, replied that Franklin did not know what he was talking about. The union between England and Scotland had been an "incorporating," not a "federal union." Nothing, he said, relating to individuals could ever come before Congress, while Roger Sherman replied that "we ought not to vote according to numbers. We are representatives of states, not individuals."[53]

In the end only the Virginians kept up the fight for voting according to population, but, as in the first Congress, the small states had the votes. Ten years later some of the same men, including James Wilson and Roger Sherman, using most of the same arguments, renewed the debate in the Convention of 1787. There the debate became so heated that at one point the delegates of the large states considered withdrawing from the convention and creating a constitution for themselves.

A second provision of the Dickinson draft produced a confrontation between the North and the South, and a debate which, like that over representation, was a prelude to an even more bitter debate in the Convention of 1787. The issue was slavery. Dickinson proposed that expenses be shared among the states according to the total number of inhabitants of every age, sex, and quality except for Indians not paying taxes. That meant that slaves would be counted, and the South objected. Samuel Chase of Maryland moved that expenses be shared on the basis of white population only. Slaves were wealth and a species of personal property. If southern property were to be taxed, why not the mercantile wealth of New England? Edward Rutledge added that the New England states would become "the carriers of the southern" and acquire wealth that would not be taxed.

Rutledge thus raised what was to become one of the most divisive issues of the 1780's when the New Englanders tried to give Congress power to regulate trade. The southerners blocked the attempt because they were convinced that New England shippers would secure a monopoly which would mean higher freight rates and lower profits for southern planters.

John Adams tried to avoid the issue by arguing that total population was the best index of wealth and that it made no difference whether labor was slave or free. But James Wilson, as in the Convention of 1787, antagonized southerners. He told Congress that slaves ate the food of freemen and that the southerners should free their slaves and hire free labor. Thomas Lynch of South Carolina replied that if it were debated "whether their slaves are their property, there is an end of confederation." Slaves were property and they should not be taxed any more than land, sheep, cattle, and horses. Benjamin Franklin did not cool tempers by answering that slaves weakened the state and that there was a difference between them and sheep since "sheep will never make any insurrections." Chase's motion to share expenses according to white population was rejected on a straight sectional vote. Delaware, Maryland, Virginia, and the two Carolinas voted for it but the seven northern states voted against it. Chase then threatened that Maryland would never agree to a confederation if slaves were counted.

Congress deadlocked on the issue and, as with representation, put off the question for over a year. By October 1777 the New Englanders stood alone for sharing expenses according to total population. Most southerners would have preferred wealth as a basis, but when that could not be obtained, the southern states voted solidly for sharing expenses according to the value of all lands granted to or surveyed for individuals. Thus the southerners escaped paying taxes on their slaves, and on their large areas of unsurveyed and ungranted lands as well.

New Englanders believed that their interests had been sacrificed. New England was relatively well settled and land was higher priced than in the South. A New Hampshire delegate declared that the southerners were escaping taxes on a third of their wealth—their slaves—and that they had a further advantage in that the quotas of troops supplied by the states were based on white population alone. Thus, he said, the slaves would be left at home and "they can till their lands and get bread and riches, while some other states may be greatly distressed."[54]

The most divisive issue of all in writing the Articles of Confederation was the control of land on the frontiers. The conflict was between the states with charter claims extending to the "South Seas" and the five states with fixed boundaries: Pennsylvania, Maryland, New Jersey, Delaware, and

Rhode Island. People in the landless states believed that the states with western claims would have an unfair advantage in paying wartime debts, but land speculators were at least as important in determining the behavior of the delegates from those states in Congress.

People of all kinds and conditions indulged in land speculation as they tried to stake out claims beyond the Appalachians in advance of settlement. English politicians and bankers and American merchants, planters, small farmers, and clergymen alike took part. It is possible that there were Members of Congress who were not speculators, but it is far easier to list those who were than to identify the few who were not. Among those from the landless states who were, Benjamin Franklin was preeminent, but James Wilson, Samuel Chase, Robert Morris, Samuel Wharton, and Charles Carroll of Carrollton were not far behind.

The problem for such men was how to circumvent Virginia's charter claims. Franklin had begun early, for the Albany Plan of Union implied that the government would have the power to limit western boundaries. Another way was to appeal to a higher authority, and Franklin spent years in England trying to persuade British authorities to create the colony of Vandalia within Virginia's charter limits. Others created land companies based on a legal opinion, which speculators altered to read that Indians, as sovereign nations, could grant lands within Virginia. The onset of the Revolution ended hopes of British help, so the speculators turned to the Continental Congress armed with shares of stock to distribute among the members. The Virginians, adept speculators themselves, made plans to distribute the lands among Virginians.

The Dickinson draft gave hope to the landless states and their speculators. Among the "sole and exclusive" powers of Congress were the power to regulate the Indian trade, to limit the bounds of the states claiming to extend to the South Seas, to fix the boundaries of states where they seemed indefinite, to establish new states in the lands separated from old states, and to sell such lands for the benefit of all the states. Dickinson evidently realized what would follow, for he attached a note to his draft: "These clauses are submitted to Congress."

Whatever the abstract merits of the provisions, the landed states would not tolerate them. When Thomas Jefferson declared that the limits of the southern states were fixed, Samuel Chase of Maryland replied that it was the "intention of some gentlemen to limit the boundaries of particular states. No colony has a right to go to the South Sea. They never had— they can't have. It would not be safe for the rest. It would be destructive of her sisters, and to herself." James Wilson declared the charter grants extravagant and the result of mistakes. "They were ignorant of geography. They thought the South Sea within 100 miles of the Atlantic Ocean." Pennsylvania had a right to say that she would interfere with those claims and a right to say that she would not confederate unless they were cut off. Jefferson had the last word: "I protest the right of Congress to decide upon the right of Virginia," and he added with more smugness or arrogance than tact that Virginia, in its recently adopted constitution, had ceded its claims to the land now occupied by Maryland, Pennsylvania, and the two Carolinas.

Congress dropped the provisions giving it power over land and boundaries in August 1776. The landless states continued the struggle, but they failed to restore those powers in October 1777. The landed states then protected their claims when Richard Henry Lee inserted, at the end of a provision for settling disputes over lands, the guarantee that "no state shall be deprived of territory for the benefit of the United States."

★ ★ ★

The disagreements over representation, sharing of expenses, and control of the west resulted in shifting alliances among states and regions according to their interests. The dispute over the west raised the issue of the power of the central government over the states, but the question of sovereignty as a principle remained undecided.

For a time, a deadlocked Congress abandoned the effort to complete a constitution. Congress had other and more pressing problems, for mounting military disasters posed the question of the survival of Congress itself. Congress fled from Philadelphia to Baltimore at the end of 1776, returned to Philadelphia, and then fled across the Susquehanna River to York, Pa. There, in November 1777, Congress finally completed the Articles of Confederation.

The final constitution was derived from Dickinson's draft, but as James Wilson told the Convention in 1787, "The original draft of confederation" was based on the idea of Congress as a single state, "and the draft concluded on how different!"[55] The issue of the fundamental nature of the constitution was raised in Congress by men who tried to establish precedents for the exercise of congressional power over the states and their citizens. They were men long accustomed to the use of sophisticated legal and constitutional ideas, but so too were the men who opposed them. The debate over precedents divided Congress according to basic political convictions rather than regional or state interests, and the result reversed the intent of the Dickinson draft.

The idea of establishing precedents for centralized power antedated the Declaration of Independence. In the spring of 1775, when James Rivington attacked Congress in his newspaper, New York referred the case to the Congress. Gouverneur Morris urged Richard Henry Lee to support action by Congress, "for it is the giving a new power to Congress. Our Association hath given them the legislative, and this now tenders them the judicial supremacy. The power of government, as of man, is to be collected from small instances; great affairs are more the objects of reflection and policy. Here both join."[56]

Morris also saw, earlier than most, the political significance of centralized control of finance. He told the New York Provincial Congress in 1775 that the Continental Congress should have complete control of paper money because, aside from the economics involved, it would "provide a new bond of union" among the colonies by "creating a common interest in the property of the circulating medium, and a common responsibility for its final redemption."[57] This was six years before Alexander Hamilton described a national debt as a national blessing and an essential cement to the union, and before another Morris, Robert of Philadelphia, used financial power in an attempt to acquire political power for Congress during the closing years of the War for Independence.[58]

However, a serious attempt to establish precedents was not made until 1777.[59] The leader of the attempt was James Wilson, who from 1776 onward was one of the most consistent supporters of a powerful central government. In December 1776 the New England states held a convention and sent an account of their proceedings to Congress. Wilson wrote a report approving the convention, the purpose being "that this approbation might imply a right to disapprove."

Samuel Adams and Richard Henry Lee denied that Congress had any power to act. Adams told Congress "that a right to assemble upon all occasions to consult measures for promoting liberty and happiness was the privilege of freemen—that it was contested by Governor Hutchinson and that it was dreaded only by tyrants." James Wilson replied that since the business of the convention was wholly continental, it required the approval of Congress. So too did John Adams, who argued that the states had no right to touch upon continental subjects. Benjamin Rush went so far as to insist that the convention had usurped the powers of Congress. Congress at first approved the convention, but later it conceded that Congress had no authority over the states.

Then General Washington created a storm when, on January 25, 1777, he issued a proclamation requiring all those who had taken an oath of allegiance to Britain to take an oath of allegiance to the United States or be treated as common enemies. The proclamation raised the question: was there national citizenship as well as state citizenship? When the news reached Congress, Abraham Clark of New Jersey moved a resolution to prevent "its fatal consequences and the establishing such a precedent." No matter what Congress did, he wrote the Speaker of the New Jersey House of Representatives, New Jersey should "not tamely submit their authority to the control of a power unknown in our constitution; we set out to oppose tyranny in all its strides, and I hope we shall persevere." Clark later called the proclamation " a violation of our civil rights" and reported that opposition was so strong that Congress refused to act on a committee report favorable to Washington's proclamation.

Simultaneously another question "concerning the jurisdiction of Congress and the states" arose over a proposed amendment to a report on desertion. The report recommended that the states pass laws authorizing constables and other officials to pick up deserters from the Continental Army. The amendment would allow Congress to bypass the states and authorize local officials to pick up deserters and deliver them to Continental officers. Congress adopted the amendment and the debate began. The two leading contenders were Scottish-born James Wilson and Irish-born Thomas Burke, who had arrived in Congress as a delegate from North Carolina.

Burke demanded reconsideration of the amendment. Wilson argued that desertion was a continental matter and therefore Congress had the power to intervene directly without consulting the states. Burke replied that if Congress had the power to enforce its provisions, it would have the power to prostrate state laws and constitutions and create within the states an authority that could act independently of them. Such a power would destroy the barriers erected by the states for the security of their citizens. The citizen of a state was entitled to the protection of his state and "subject to the laws of that alone, because to them alone did he give his consent." If Congress had the power to pick up deserters, then it had "power unlimited over the lives and liberties of all men in America." The amendment was defeated.

An attempt to change the rules of Congress aroused an equally intense debate. Some members of Congress wanted to leave Baltimore and return to Philadelphia, but others opposed such a move. James Wilson and John Adams argued that a majority of the members of Congress, rather than a majority of the states, could decide whether the rule of "one state, one vote" applied. Richard Henry Lee denounced the idea as a "violent impropriety," while Thomas Burke refused to debate the matter but made a long speech in opposition. If the majority could vote away rules agreed to by common consent, Congress was "bound by no rule at all and only governed by arbitrary discretion." If such an "arbitrary tyrannical discretion" was exercised, Burke would regard it as a violent invasion of the rights of North Carolina. Congress could no longer be trusted with the liberties of Burke's fellow citizens, and he would withdraw from Congress. His threat to withdraw killed the attempt to change the rules.

The futile attempt to establish precedents for congressional power over the states and their citizens raised the fundamental issue of sovereignty, and the man who forced Congress to face the issue was Thomas Burke. He concluded after the debates, echoing English republican writers, that "the more experience I acquire the stronger is my conviction that *unlimited power cannot be safely trusted* to any man or set of men on earth." He asked: What can induce members of Congress to increase their power? He answered: "This is a question I believe cannot be answered but by a plain declaration that power of all kinds has an irresistible propensity to increase a desire for itself. It gives the passion of ambition a velocity which increases in proportion as it is gratified."[60]

Burke's opportunity to put his convictions, and those of other Revolutionary leaders, in constitutional form came when Congress resumed consideration of the Articles of Confederation in April 1777. Burke read the third article of the Dickinson draft and found that it "expressed only a reservation of the power of regulating the internal police, and consequently resigned every other power." He said that the article "left it in the power of the future Congress or General Council to explain away every right belonging to the states and to make their own power as unlimited as they please." Burke therefore proposed an amendment, which, he said, "held up the principle that all sovereign power was in the states separately, and that particular acts of it, which should be expressly enumerated, would be exercised in conjunction, and not otherwise; but that in all things else each state would exercise all the rights and power of sovereignty uncontrolled." Burke reported that his motion was so little understood at first that it did not receive a second, but eventually 11 states voted for it.[61]

The amendment, the second article of the Articles of Confederation, reads: "Each State retains its sovereignty, freedom and independence, and every power, jurisdiction, and right, which is not by this confederation expressly delegated to the United States, in Congress assembled."

The words "expressly delegated" were the heart of the constitutional matter. A decade later one state convention after another proposed to add the second article of the Articles of Confederation as an amendment to the Constitution. The Massachusetts amendment was concise: "that it be explicitly declared that all powers not expressly delegated by the aforesaid Constitution are reserved to the several states to be by them exercised." The demand for such an amendment was so powerful that James Madison included it in the amendments he offered to Congress in June 1789. But his version was ambiguous and indirect and omitted the word "expressly." Two Antifederalist members of the House, Thomas Tudor Tucker of South Carolina and Elbridge Gerry of Massachusetts, tried and failed to add the word "expressly." What became the tenth amendment to the Constitution reads: "The powers not delegated to the United States by the Constitution, nor prohibited by it to the States, are reserved to the States respectively, or to the people."

The men at the time understood the implications of the word "expressly" in the Articles of Confederation and the refusal to insert it in the tenth amendment to the Constitution. To them that single word was no mere quibble. It embodied two broadly different conceptions of the rightful balance of power between the central government and the governments of the states.

★ ★ ★

On November 17, 1777, Congress sent the Articles of Confederation to the states for the required unanimous ratification, accompanied by a letter summing up the problems it had faced. "This business," Congress declared,

> equally intricate and important, has in its progress, been attended with uncommon embarrassments and delay, which the most anxious solicitude and persevering diligence could not prevent. To form a permanent union, accommodated to the opinion and wishes of the delegates of so many states, differing in habits, produce, commerce, and internal police, was found to be a work which nothing but time and reflection, conspiring with a disposition to conciliate, could mature and accomplish.
>
> Hardly is it to be expected that any plan, in the variety of provisions essential to our union, should exactly correspond with the maxims and political views of every particular state.[62]

The states responded as their delegates had done in the debates on the Articles in Congress. Virginia ratified first and without amendments, but grave doubts had been raised by Congress' treatymaking power. At the last minute Richard Henry Lee had secured an addition to the Articles. It forbade Congress to make commercial treaties preventing the states from levying the same duties on foreigners that their own citizens were subject to, and preventing the states from prohibiting the exportation or importation of any goods whatsoever. Nevertheless, some Virginians feared that the states "which have not a staple"—that is, the northern states—might grant monopolies at the expense of the southern states in exchange for commercial privileges for themselves. They were assured that the second article of the Confederation meant that Congress could exercise only "expressly delegated" powers, but the fear remained that "at some future day such a power would be assumed."[63]

The Articles received far more intensive consideration in South Carolina, which offered more than 20 amendments. William Henry Drayton told the legislature that "the second article speaks of the sovereignty of the respective states, but by the time we arrive at the last, scarce the shadow of sovereignty remains." Like the Virginians, he feared that future congresses would find what they wanted in the "spirit of the law" and interpret the Confederation to suit their interests. Above all, he predicted, the South would be exploited by the North. The prospect was that the nine northern states would control Congress "contrary to the united opposition of Virginia, the two Carolinas, and Georgia: states possessing more than half of the whole territory of the confederacy . . . and forming the body of the southern interest. If things of such transcendent weight, may be done notwithstanding such an opposition, the honor, interest, and sovereignty of the South, are in effect delivered up to the care of the North. Do we intend to make such a surrender? I hope not. There is no occasion for it."[64] Ten years later to the month, Rawlins Lowndes made a similar speech to the South Carolina legislature criticizing the Constitution written by the Convention of 1787.

In the North, New Hampshire and Massachusetts submitted the Articles to the towns of the two states. New Hampshire towns objected to sharing expenses according to land values. Some Massachusetts towns wanted personal property and income added to the tax base. Others thought that declaring war and making peace should be left to the people, not to Congress. However, these two states, along with Connecticut and Rhode Island, authorized their delegates to ratify if amendments could not be agreed upon.

Congress rejected all proposed amendments, and by January 1779, 12 states had signed the Articles of Confederation. Only Maryland refused, and it continued to refuse for more than two years thereafter. Maryland declared it would not ratify until Congress was given the power to limit charter claims and define state boundaries, and until Congress recognized Maryland's right to a share in the lands lying "westward of the frontiers of the United States," lands not granted to individuals before the war.

The central issue was the "lands granted to individuals," that is, the lands claimed by speculators of the landless states. In 1779 Virginia declared void all land company claims within her charter limits and opened a land office to sell the land to Virginians. The land companies then petitioned Congress to stop Virginia. The debate which followed disrupted Congress during some of the darkest days of the War for Independence. In the course of it, one of the companies proposed a novel constitutional doctrine. An Indiana Company petition declared that *"all the rights and all the obligations of the Crown of Great Britain* respecting the lands and governments herein before mentioned devolve upon the *United States* and are to be claimed, exercised, and discharged by the United States in Congress assembled."[65]

Virginia denied Congress' right to interfere, and the abstract doctrine of the devolution of sovereignty heightened fears that the Articles of Confederation had not been careful enough in defining the limits of congressional power. In the end, Virginia ceded the Old Northwest to Congress, but required Congress to nullify all speculative claims in the area.[66]

The cession did not end disputes over land, for such disputes, like political ideas of the highest order, were an integral part of the history of the Revolutionary era, as they were of American history for years thereafter. But the Virginia cession at last brought Maryland to ratify the Articles of Confederation on March 1, 1781. They thus became the constitution of the United States only a few months before the effective end of the War for Independence.

★ ★ ★

The Articles of Confederation were written by men shortly after they declared an independence they had not yet achieved, and at a time when there was no guarantee that they ever would. They were written by men who had to spend most of their time in a desperate effort to support a war against the greatest military and naval power on earth, and to support it without funds, without supplies, without competent generals, and without enough soldiers who had the means, and sometimes the will, to fight. By any objective standard, the men who wrote the Articles were either incurably mad or incredibly optimistic, or perhaps a mixture of both.

The Articles reflected the political ideology of the leaders who dominated the early years of the Revolutionary era. They also reflected the diversity of political and social attitudes and economic interests of the various states, but at the same time demonstrated the capacity of the Revolutionary leaders to compromise or submerge those differences in their determination to create a common government.

The Articles of Confederation, as a constitution, were only a way station on the road to another constitution, but that did not mean that some Americans abandoned their belief that a truly federal government of sovereign states was the best government for a diverse nation. They would not have agreed with Governor Edmund Randolph's speech opening the Convention in 1787 "in which he pointed out the various defects of the federal system, the necessity of transforming it into a national, efficient government. . . ."[67] Samuel Adams did not hear the speech, but when he read the Constitution, he wrote his old friend Richard Henry Lee: "I confess as I enter the building I stumble at the threshold. I meet with a national government instead of a federal union of sovereign states."[68]

Convictions such as those of Samuel Adams and Richard Henry Lee did much to shape the Articles of Confederation, to restrain the men in the Convention of 1787 who wanted to destroy the states as political entities, and to shape the character and quality of American political life for years after 1787.

In many and various ways, therefore, the Articles of Confederation were one of the fundamental testaments of the American Revolution.

Notes

[1] William Waller Hening, ed., *The Statutes at Large; Being a Collection of the Laws of Virginia, From the First Session of the Legislature, in the Year 1619*, 13 vols. (New York: R., W. and G. Bartow, 1809–23), 1:124. The law was repassed several times, and the council, as well as the governor, was forbidden to levy taxes without the consent of the assembly. Ibid., 1:171, 196, 244.

The quotations in this essay are presented in modern form, except where capital letters or italics were evidently used for emphasis.

[2] Nathaniel B. Shurtleff, ed., *Records of the Governor and Company of the Massachusetts Bay in New England*, 5 vols. (Boston: William White, printer to the Commonwealth, 1853–54), 5:200.

[3] Merrill Jensen, ed., *American Colonial Documents to 1776*, English Historical Documents, vol. 9 (London and New York: Eyre & Spottiswoode and Oxford University Press, 1955), pp. 672–73.

4 Francis Bernard to Lord Barrington, November 23, 1765, in Edward Channing and Archibald Cary Coolidge, eds., *The Barrington-Bernard Correspondence* (Cambridge: Harvard University Press, 1912), p. 96.

5 "Age & Experience," *Boston Gazette,* January 11, 1773.

6 "Americanus," *New York Journal,* November 11, 1773.

7 "Hampden," No. II, *Virginia Gazette* (Purdie and Dixon), November 11, 1773.

8 "Z," *Boston Gazette,* October 11, 1773.

9 Andrew Burnaby, *Travels Through the Middle Settlements in North America* . . . (2d London ed., 1775; reprint ed., Ithaca: Cornell University Press, 1960), pp. 113–14.

10 William Gordon, *The History of the Rise, Progress and Establishment of the Independence of the United States of America* . . . , 4 vols. (London: Printed for the author, 1788), 1:394.

11 Adams to Hezekiah Niles, February 13, 1818, in Charles F. Adams, ed., *The Works of John Adams* . . . , 10 vols. (Boston: Little, Brown and Co., 1850–56), 10:283.

12 "Coriolanus," *New York Gazette,* August 27, 1770.

13 John Adams Diary, August 22, 1774, in L. H. Butterfield, ed., *Diary and Autobiography of John Adams,* 4 vols. (Cambridge: Harvard University Press, 1961), 2:107.

14 Alvah Hovey, *A Memoir of the Life and Times of the Rev. Isaac Backus, A.M.* (Boston: Gould and Lincoln, 1859), pp. 204–12.

15 Adams, Diary, August 23, 1774, *Diary and Autobiography,* 2:109.

16 Adams, Diary, October 9, 1774, ibid., 2:150.

17 Adams to Joseph Hawley, November 25, 1775, in *Works of John Adams,* 9:366–67.

18 John Adams to Abigail Adams, September 16, 1774, in L. H. Butterfield, ed., *Adams Family Correspondence,* 2 vols. (Cambridge: Harvard University Press, 1963), 1:156; Adams, Diary, September 10, 1774, *Diary and Autobiography,* 2:131.

19 Adams to James Warren, [July] 6, 1775, in Worthington C. Ford, ed., *Warren-Adams Letters,* 2 vols. (Boston: Massachusetts Historical Society, 1917–25), 1:76–77.

20 Washington to Lund Washington, August 20, 1775, in John C. Fitzpatrick, ed., *The Writings of George Washington,* 39 vols. (Washington: United States Government Printing Office, 1931–44), 3:433.

21 *New York Journal,* October 6, 1768; reprinted in the *Boston Gazette,* October 24, 1768.

22 Robert Yates, Notes on Debates, June 18, 1787, in Max Farrand, ed., *The Records of the Federal Convention of 1787,* 3 vols. (New Haven: Yale University Press, 1911), 1:299.

23 John Tucker, *A Sermon Preached in Cambridge* . . . (Boston, 1771), p. 34.

24 *Considerations on the Present State of Virginia* (n.p., 1774). Reprinted in Earl G. Swem, ed., *Virginia and the Revolution: Two Pamphlets: 1774* (New York: Charles F. Heartman, 1919), pp. 15, 17.

25 Morris to John Penn, May 20, 1774, in Jared Sparks, *The Life of Gouverneur*

Morris . . . , 3 vols. (Boston: Gray and Bowen, 1832), 1:23-26.

[26] The fullest documentation of the Albany Plan is in Leonard W. Labaree et al., eds., *The Papers of Benjamin Franklin* (New Haven: Yale University Press, 1959-), 5:344-53, 357-92, 397-415.

[27] Printed in Hampton L. Carson, ed., *History of the Celebration of the One Hundredth Anniversary . . . of the Constitution of the United States*, 2 vols. (Philadelphia: J. B. Lippincott Company, 1889), 2:482-86.

[28] Sparks, *Life of Morris*, 1:26-27. The passage cited is Sparks' summary. Sparks does not print the essay.

[29] Wharton to Thomas Walpole, May 2 and 31, 1774, and to Samuel Wharton, July 5, 1774, Thomas Wharton Letterbook, 1773-1784, pp. 34-35, 45-46, 50-51, Historical Society of Pennsylvania.

[30] This account is based on John Adams, Notes of Debates, September 28, 1774, in *Diary and Autobiography*, 2:141-44, 3:309; [Joseph Galloway], *A Candid Examination of the Mutual Claims of Great Britain, And the Colonies: With A Plan of Accommodation on Constitutional Principles* (New York: 1775); reprinted in Merrill Jensen, ed., *Tracts of the American Revolution 1763-1776* (Indianapolis: Bobbs-Merrill, 1967); and Joseph Galloway, *Historical and Political Reflections on the Rise and Progress of the American Rebellion* (London, 1780; reprinted with an introduction by Merrill Jensen, Johnson Reprint Corporation, New York, 1972).

[31] *A Candid Examination* . . . , in Jensen, ed., *Tracts*, p. 374. Galloway's constitution provided for an American parliament elected by the colonial legislatures and presided over by a "president general" appointed by the Crown. Each colony was to retain control of its "internal police," but all questions involving more than one colony or the colonies and Britain were to be the domain of the American parliament. Either the American or the British parliament could originate legislation concerning both Britain and America, but both bodies had to adopt a law before it could become effective.

[32] James Madison, Notes on Debates, June 29, 1787, in Farrand, ed., *Records of the Federal Convention*, 1:463-64.

[33] Secretary Josiah Willard to William Bollan, December 31, 1754, in A. B. Hart, ed., *Commonwealth History of Massachusetts*, 5 vols. (New York: The States History Company, 1928), 2:461. Both houses approved the letter.

[34] January 17, 1755. *A Report of the Record Commissioners of the City of Boston Containing the Boston Town Records, 1742-1757* (Boston: Rockwell and Churchill, City Printers, 1885), p. 266.

[35] Adams to Elbridge Gerry, October 29, 1775, in H. A. Cushing, ed., *The Writings of Samuel Adams*, 4 vols. (New York: G. P. Putnam's Sons, 1904-08), 3:229.

[36] Peter Force, ed., *American Archives* . . . , 4th Series, 6 vols. (Washington: Published by M. St. Clair Clarke and Peter Force, Under Authority of an Act of Congress . . . 1833, 1837-46), 6:1,524.

[37] Pittsfield Petition to the House of Representatives, May 29, 1776, in Robert J. Taylor, ed., *Massachusetts, Colony to Commonwealth: Documents on the Formation of Its Constitution, 1775-1780* (Chapel Hill: University of North Carolina Press, 1961), pp. 26-29.

38 Alexander Hamilton, "The Continentalist," No. I, in *The Papers of Alexander Hamilton*, ed. Harold C. Syrett et al. (New York: Columbia University Press, 1961-), 2:649-52.

39 November 9, 1775. Force, ed., *American Archives*, 4th ser., 3:1,793.

40 June 28, 1775. Ibid., 2:1,329.

41 Braxton to Landon Carter, April 14, 1776, in Edmund C. Burnett, ed., *Letters of Members of the Continental Congress*, 8 vols. (Washington: Carnegie Institution of Washington, 1921-36), 1:421.

42 Carter to George Washington, May 9, 1776, in Force, ed., *American Archives*, 4th ser., 6:390.

43 Adams to James Warren, April 22, 1776, in *Warren-Adams Letters*, 1:233-34.

44 Adams to John Winthrop, June 23, 1776, in Massachusetts Historical Society, *Collections*, 5th ser., vol. 4 (1878), p. 310.

45 Adams to James Warren, May 20, 1776, in *Warren-Adams Letters*, 1:249-51. For a more detailed account of events in 1775-76, see Merrill Jensen, *The Founding of a Nation: A History of the American Revolution 1763-1776* (New York: Oxford University Press, 1968), chap. 24.

46 Adams to Patrick Henry, June 3, 1776, in Burnett, ed., *Letters*, 1:471.

47 In Jensen, ed., *American Colonial Documents to 1776*, p. 876.

48 Rutledge to John Jay, June 29, 1776, in Burnett, ed., *Letters*, 1:517-18.

49 Secretary Josiah Willard to William Bollan, December 31, 1754, in Hart, ed., *Commonwealth History of Massachusetts*, 2:461.

50 Gordon to John Adams, September 7, 1782, "Letters of the Reverend William Gordon, Historian of the Revolution, 1770-1799," in Massachusetts Historical Society, *Proceedings* 63 (1929-30): 469.

51 Louis B. Wright, ed., *An Essay Upon the Government of the English Plantations on the Continent of America (1701)* . . . (San Marino, Cal.: The Huntington Library, 1945).

52 John Adams, Notes on Debates, September 5 and 6, 1774, *Diary and Autobiography*, 2:123-26.

53 For the notes on the debates in July and August 1776 from which these quotations are taken, see John Adams, Notes on Debates, *Diary and Autobiography*, 2:241-50, and Thomas Jefferson, Notes on Proceedings in the Continental Congress, June 7-August 1, 1776, *The Papers of Thomas Jefferson*, ed. Julian P. Boyd et al. (Princeton: Princeton University Press, 1950-), 1:320-27. For a detailed account upon which the foregoing and following accounts of the writing of the Articles of Confederation are based, see Merrill Jensen, *The Articles of Confederation: An Interpretation of the Social-Constitutional History of the American Revolution 1774-1781* (Madison: University of Wisconsin Press, 1940).

54 Nathaniel Folsom to President Meshech Weare of New Hampshire, November 21, 1777, in Burnett, ed., *Letters*, 2:564.

[55] Robert Yates, Notes on Debates, June 8, 1787, in Farrand, ed., *Records of the Federal Convention*, 1:170.

[56] New York, May 1775 in Force, ed., *American Archives*, 4th ser., 2:726. Lee either did not see the point or ignored it. See Lee to Morris, May 28, 1775, ibid.

[57] Sparks, *Life of Morris*, 1:38-39.

[58] See E. James Ferguson, *The Power of the Purse* (Chapel Hill: University of North Carolina Press, 1961) for an explication of the interrelationship of economic and political power as understood by men of the Revolutionary generation.

[59] For the debates on the attempt to establish precedents, see Benjamin Rush Diary, February 4, 1777, in Burnett, ed., *Letters*, 2:234-35; Abraham Clark to John Hart, February 8, 1777, ibid., pp. 242-44; Clark to Elias Dayton, March 7, 1777, ibid., pp. 291-92; and Thomas Burke, Abstract of Debates, February 25 and 26, ibid., pp. 275-81, 282-84.

[60] Burke to Governor Richard Caswell of North Carolina, March 11, 1777, ibid., p. 294.

[61] Burke to Governor Richard Caswell, April 29, 1777, ibid., pp. 345-46.

[62] U.S. Continental Congress, *Journals of the Continental Congress, 1774-1789*, ed. Worthington C. Ford et al., 34 vols. (Washington: Library of Congress, 1904-37), 9:933.

[63] Thomas Jefferson to John Adams, December 17, 1777, in Boyd, ed., *Papers of Thomas Jefferson*, 2:120-21.

[64] Drayton, speech to the South Carolina Legislature, January 20, 1777, in Hezekiah Niles, ed., *Principles and Acts of the Revolution in America* . . . , rev. ed. (New York, Chicago, and New Orleans: A. S. Barnes & Co., 1876), pp. 357-64. Drayton also presented the legislature with a much more detailed and precise version of "Articles of Confederation" which he had written, ibid., pp. 364-74.

[65] Papers of the Continental Congress, No. 77, ff. 234-36, National Archives.

[66] For a detailed account of the land companies and Congress, see Jensen, *Articles of Confederation*, pp. 198-238.

[67] Madison, Notes on Debates, May 29, 1787, in Farrand, ed., *Records of the Federal Convention*, 1:18, n. 7.

[68] Adams to Lee, December 3, 1787, in Cushing, ed., *Writings of Samuel Adams*, 4:324.

MERRILL JENSEN, Vilas Research Professor of History at the University of Wisconsin, is the author of *The Articles of Confederation* (1940, 1947, 1959) and *The New Nation: A History of the United States During the Confederation, 1781–1789* (1950), which was chosen by the History Book Club as book-of-the-month in December 1950. His other publications have included *Regionalism in America* (1941), *American Colonial Documents to 1776* (Volume 9 of *English Historical Documents*, 1955), an introduction to a new edition of R. G. Adams' *Political Ideas of the American Revolution* (1957), *The Making of the American Constitution* (1964), and *The Founding of a Nation* (1968). In 1964 three of his books were chosen for the White House library. Currently he is editing *The Documentary History of the First Federal Elections* for the National Historical Publications Commission. In 1970 he became editor of *The Documentary History of the Ratification of the Constitution*.

After receiving B.A. (1929) and M.A. (1931) degrees at the University of Washington and a Ph.D. degree (1934) at the University of Wisconsin, Professor Jensen joined the History Department at the University of Washington, where he taught from 1935 to 1944. He was also managing editor of the *Pacific Northwest Quarterly* from 1935 to 1942 and served as historian with the U.S. Army Air Force in 1944. He accepted an appointment as associate professor of history at the University of Wisconsin in 1944 and was promoted to the rank of professor in 1947. He became chairman of the History Department in 1961, a position which he held until 1964, when he was named to the Vilas Research Professorship.

Professor Jensen has been concerned with the development of American studies overseas for many years. In 1949–50 he was Harmsworth Professor of American History at the University of Oxford. In 1955 he gave a seminar on American history at the University of Tokyo, and in 1960 he gave a seminar on American colonial history at the University of Ghent. He also conducted three series of seminars at Kyoto University, in 1961, 1964, and 1971.

Professor Jensen's professional affiliations include membership in the American Historical Association and the Organization of American Historians, of which he was president in 1969–70. He has served on the editorial boards of *The Mississippi Valley Historical Review* (now *The Journal of American History*) and the *American Quarterly*.

We now come to the conclusion of the war, the Treaty of Paris of 1783. Two weeks ago I had the pleasure of taking part in a testimonial dinner in honor of Professor Richard B. Morris, Gouverneur Morris Professor of History at Columbia, on the occasion of his retirement. I hailed him then as being—since the departure of Lawrence Gipson from the scene—our senior colonial historian, King Richard the Steadfast, successor to King Gipson the Venerable. But unlike Gipson, Professor Morris has not been a disciple of any school or a founder of one. He has done something better. He has been, as I indicated on that occasion, a builder of bridges—bridges across chasms that need to be crossed in the exploration of the past. First of all, with his remarkable doctoral dissertation on American colonial legal practices, he led social historians over into that realm of legal history where so many of us are unequipped to follow him. He has built bridges between the archivists and the historians, now needed more than ever. He has built bridges between the generations and across other chasms.

Like Professor Jensen, Professor Morris is a scholar who grounds his work solidly on the sources—and both men teach their graduate students to do the same. In 1965, when his The Peacemakers, *the account of the Treaty of Paris negotiations, came out, the* New York Times *had this to say:*

> It is astonishing that an event so fateful in its effect on the destiny of empires, so dramatic in its momentous conflict of interests and ideals, so instinct with almost every form of human ambition, jealousy, deception, and roguery, as well as courage, generosity, sagacity and honor, should have waited until now for a Mattingly or a Morison to do it justice. The great theme, to be sure, has been ably and searchingly treated from various points of view by scholars here and abroad. But these studies, valuable as they are, have always been incidental to some general or specialized work of biography or of diplomatic, political, economic, or military history. The full story, in all of its challenging and dramatic amplitude, like Benjamin West's famous group portrait of the signing of the preliminary treaty of 1782, has remained tantalizingly incomplete. Now, at last, a master of the historian's craft worthy of the challenge has appeared.

The Peacemakers, *in the opinion of many of us—including myself, who wrote the remarks I have just quoted—should have received the Pulitzer award. It did receive the Bancroft prize, which it fully deserved, and established Professor Morris as* the *authority on the Treaty of Paris.*

The Treaty of Paris of 1783

RICHARD B. MORRIS

BY ANY STANDARDS, the Definitive Treaty negotiated between Great Britain and the United States in Paris and signed on September 3, 1783,[1] was an extraordinary document, whether measured by such criteria as the revolutionary objectives of the American negotiators, the very peculiar and complex nature of the bargaining, the relevance of the negotiations to today's diplomacy in several critical areas, or the durable character of the treaty itself.

Where today are the Treaties of Utrecht of 1713, of Paris of 1763, of Hubertusburg of the same year, or of Kuchuk Kainarji of the year following? They are all ghosts of a vanished past, along with the Spanish, the Dutch, the French, the Turkish, and the British empires, with the departed but not mourned Bourbons, Hapsburgs, Hohenzollerns, Romanovs, and Ottoman sultans. True, Britain grimly grips the Rock of Gibraltar, but if the slave trade, over which Utrecht conferred special privileges upon the British, has been superseded by the illegal traffic in narcotics, no one nation seems to have been awarded the *asiento*. Instead of monopoly, we are offered the scandalous spectacle of covert competition. The Turks have long been ousted from the Crimea and much else, Austria's multilingual dominion in the days of Maria Theresa and Joseph II is a mere fragment of its past glory, and much of Prussia has slid off the map of either of the Germanies, neither of which is likely to engage in a war over the Bavarian succession.

If the map of Europe has been altered beyond all recognition since the American and French Revolutions and if the old empires which managed to survive down to the last generation have been superseded by emerging

Copyright 1973 by Richard B. Morris

nations since 1945, one might confidently assert that the present bounds of the continental United States were an inevitable outcome of the territorial gains achieved at Paris in the fall of 1782. That Americans would increase, multiply, and expand seemed a grim likelihood to the rulers of Spain, and it quickly became clear that no European power was in a position to curb them. Having secured generous boundaries, limits which exceeded by far those of any previous republic, the United States, as nationalist-minded statesmen saw it, must by logic and inevitability establish very special constitutional arrangements known as federalism to ensure effective central authority over the vast domain while reserving to the states and the people powers not explicitly granted the national government.

Aside from minor details about fisheries, boundary lines, and debt settlements, all of which remained to be renegotiated over the years, the gains secured by the American commissioners at Paris formalized the recognition of the United States as an independent nation, a concession grasped from the number one power of that day. Thus, the Definitive Treaty still stands as a basic charter of our national existence, challenging statesmen to a course of innovation perhaps unrivaled in any brief period by any other nation. I refer to the two spectacular products of constitutional thinking of the years between 1784 and 1787, the Northwest Territory Ordinance and the Federal Constitution. Finally, the vast new lands to which title was now settled and presumably to be undisturbed made possible that socioeconomic upthrust which transformed America into a more democratic society than it was before the American Revolution began.

The labyrinthine negotiations and the undercover operations that preceded the successful negotiation of the treaties ending the war have been examined in detail in my book *The Peacemakers; the Great Powers and American Independence*,[2] and I shall dispense with the tales of double espionage with which that volume is replete or with reviewing the agonizing frustrations that confronted John Jay in Spain, John Adams in France and Holland, Francis Dana in Russia, and William Lee in Berlin and Vienna. In fact, the peacemaking of 1782–83 constituted three separate sets of negotiations—the first, between Great Britain and the United States; the second, between Great Britain and France, America's ally since 1778, as well as with Spain, France's ally since 1779 but not America's (and in this second series the French really confronted their Spanish ally with a fait accompli); and still a third series of negotiations conducted between Britain and the United Provinces, now better known as the Netherlands. To say nothing of the remnant of a fourth series of negotiations between Russian and Austria to dominate the peace as comediators.

What we must bear in mind, and what really constitutes the nub of the matter, is that America's quest for foreign aid and the resultant alliance with France seriously affected both the operation of the American war and the peace aims adopted and frequently reshaped by the Continental Congress. Like the Vietnam war, perhaps now subsiding, the American Revolutionary conflict posed a conundrum. How can one secure needed foreign aid without subordinating one's control of the war and one's very independence to a foreign nation or nations? The Americans were fortunate at the start, for the leading patriots put their minds to first things first— that is, to foreign aid rather than to foreign alliances. Men like John Adams warned that alliances would entangle America in future European wars—and his words were echoed in Washington's Farewell Address and in Jefferson's First Inaugural.

France hardly needed to be persuaded of the benefits to be derived from an alliance with the United States, especially after Saratoga and word of Britain's impending peace moves. To redress the balance of power thrust badly off equilibrium by the Peace of Paris of 1763 and to achieve limited peace aims, objectives which sounded increasingly avaricious in the closing moments of the war, France needed to share in America's ultimate triumph. The diplomacy of the alliance really was a race against time, with the French outdistancing the Carlisle Peace Commission and rendering the appearance of the British commissioners in America more than slightly ridiculous. What complicated the issues of peace now were the diverse interests of France and America regarding the Newfoundland fisheries, which the senior partner did not wish to share with the junior, as well as France's obvious coolness toward a second invasion of Canada. It was not in France's national interest to have the new American republic in possession of so huge a slice of the North American continent.

Complicating still further America's peace objectives was Spain's entry into the war as an ally of France but not of the United States. By the secret treaty entered into with France at Aranjuez on April 12, 1779,[3] Spain induced France to admit Spanish subjects to the fisheries in Newfoundland, which France hoped to regain, and presumably no one else, and to recover Pensacola and Mobile, lost in the previous war, while the courts bound themselves to make no peace or enter into any truce until Gibraltar should be restored to Spain. Thus if the war were now to be fought to secure for Spain both banks of the Mississippi, the issue of America's navigation of that river would seem to have been superseded by rendering the Mississippi a national (Spanish) rather than an international waterway,[4] and the pledge to continue the war until Gibraltar was regained would, technically, have kept the United States at war with England down to the present day. In short, the main Spanish war objectives—and to a lesser degree those of France—were as diametrically opposed to America's war aims as were those of the enemy she was engaged in fighting.

As a result of this double conflict of peace objectives—between the warring powers on the one hand and the United States and her ally's ally on the other—Congress devoted far more effort and expended far more bile in drafting, debating, and adopting peace objectives relating to the French and Spaniards than to the British, and, as regards America's claims to boundaries, the allies proved far more obdurate than the enemy.

This point, which historians have seldom placed in proper perspective, deserves some emphasis. It was brought home to me only recently when, in the course of preparation of testimony as an expert witness for the government in *U.S. v. Maine et al.*, a suit brought to determine the title to the continental shelf off the Atlantic coast, I had occasion once again to plow through the *Journals* and papers of the Continental Congress and to restudy the instructions of Congress to its commissioners abroad. I found that the task of disentangling specific ultimata and other desired peace objectives from resolutions embodying advice and cautions, proffered amendments, and adopted amendments constituted cruel and unusual punishment, which I thought had been barred by the eighth amendment. What struck me was that the concerns of Congress as to peace aims toward Great Britain were, save in one category, arrived at quickly and with little controversy, whereas the peace ultimata involving our ally and our ally's ally proved a source of bitter contention and division in Congress from the beginning of 1779 almost down to the moment of the ratification of the Definitive Treaty.[5]

Much ink has been spilled over John Jay's insistence on independence as a precondition to entering into peace negotiations. Vergennes considered Jay unreasonably obdurate; Franklin was indifferent to the point. When one considers Congress' initial demand, and then its realistic concession on the score of preconditions, the issue takes on a special relevance to recent events. Congress first demanded that, as a precondition to entering upon negotiations, the British army leave the 13 states,[6] but this precondition was soon dropped, and the American peacemakers never made it a precondition. They were too realistic to insist upon conditions that would be insupportable to the pride of a Great Power or that they were in fact unable to effectuate. Even after the British surrendered at Yorktown and were forced to pull their army out of the lower South, they held New York until after the signatures of the principals had been fixed to a Definitive Peace.

In fact, on this question of troop withdrawal before the final peace, it is astonishing that the point was not pressed, considering how exposed the Americans would have been had the British decided to call off the negotiations and go on with the war, holding an army of 10,000 troops in New York, in possession of Charleston, still using Halifax as a logistical base for the support of such troops, and with a navy, after Rodney's victory in the West Indies in the spring of 1782, in unchallenged command of the seas.

Thus Lord Chancellor Thurlow may have considered Jay's demands for preliminary independence to be "frivolous" and Franklin may have grumbled about "standing out for the previous acknowledgement of independency" and been overheard remarking that it was "a pity to keep three or four millions of people in war for the sake of form." Nevertheless, the fact remains that once recognition is granted it is difficult, if not impossible, to withdraw it. In recent years the long-drawn-out controversy over the shape of the conference table in Paris and the relative spots to be assigned South Vietnam and the Vietcong indicates how seriously the principal negotiators on one side or sides, as the case may have been—the United States and its South Vietnamese ally—took the issue of according recognition to revolutionary groups.

In retrospect we might fault the Revolutionary Americans for not having insisted on British withdrawal from the outlying posts as a condition precedent to final peace talks. Instead, the British troops remained, and with them the constant threat that Tories and Indians might be stirred up to renew the war. After peace came, the British army remained on the frontiers for 12 years, withdrawing only under the accumulated pressure of two military campaigns on the part of the United States and a special mission to England.

The issue of recognition raised a paramount question in American history, one that some recent constitutional writers and some pressing current litigation before the United States Supreme Court have kept very much alive. Just who or what was or were recognized in the Peace of 1783? Whom did the American peace negotiators represent, the 13 separate colonies or the United States in Congress Assembled, as the nation collectively was then called?

Technically the issue had to come up in the major treaties the United States made with France in 1778 as well as in the Preliminary Treaty with Great Britain of November 30, 1782. The Treaty of Alliance with France was made between "The Most Christian King and the United States of North America, to wit" (with the 13 states listed in geographical order).[7]

It is reasonable to regard this wording as a description of the constituent elements composing the United States, not as a series of separate treaties with each of the 13 states. Evereywhere else in the treaty, references are to "His Majesty and the said United States." In fact, article 3 refers to "the two contracting parties." The significant reference reappears in the two crucial articles of the treaty, articles 8 and 10. By the former it was agreed:

> Neither of the two parties shall conclude either truce or peace with Great Britain without the formal consent of the other first obtained; and they mutually engage not to lay down their arms until the independence of the United States shall have been formally or tacitly assured by the treaty or treaties that shall terminate the war.

Article 11 provides mutual guarantees "from the present time and forever" against all other powers of "the present possessions of the Crown of France in America, as well as those which it may acquire by the future," while "His Most Christian Majesty guarantees on his part to the United States their liberty, sovereignty and independence, absolute and unlimited, as well in matters of government as commerce, and also their possessions, and the additions or conquest that their confederation may obtain during the war, from any of the dominions now, or heretofore possessed by Great Britain in North America," which by articles 5 and 6 covered Bermuda as well. Aside from the fact that this article evades the issue of the northern, western, or southern boundaries of the United States, in all of which areas the United States did not come up to the peace conference with solid military conquests, it would seem reasonable to infer that France considered it was dealing with confederated states and not with separate states. With one dubious exception, the 13 states took the same position. That exception was Virginia. Some scholars, notably James Brown Scott, have chosen to magnify the importance of the fact that on June 2, 1779, the Virginia House of Delegates, and on the following day the Senate, ratified the treaties of alliance and commerce, significantly as "entered into between His Most Christian Majesty of France on the one part, and the Congress of the United States of America on behalf of the said states on the other part," and that Thomas Jefferson attached his signature to the ratification as governor.[8]

Little attention is paid by Mr. Scott to the fact that Jefferson some years later, in denying to the states the right to enter into foreign relations or make treaties, in effect repudiated his and his state's indiscretion in this matter. Writing to James Madison from Paris on February 8, 1785, Jefferson declared: "The politics of Europe render it indispensably necessary

The Treaty of Paris of 1783

that with respect to everything external we be one nation only, firmly hooped together. Interior government is what each state should keep to itself. . . . It should ever be held in mind that insult and war are the consequences of a want of respectability in the national character. As long as the states exercise separately those acts of power which respect foreign nations, so long will there continue to be irregularities committed by some one or other of them which will constantly keep us on an ill footing with foreign nations."[9]

Clearly in retrospect, Jefferson must have regarded the ratification of the French treaty by Virginia as an aberration, as it was so transparent a violation of the rights of Congress over foreign affairs, confirmed by article 9 of the Articles of Confederation, which gave "the United States in Congress Assembled" the sole and exclusive right to make treaties.

No such aberration occurred in the case of either the Preliminary or Definitive Treaties with Great Britain. The former was ratified by Congress on April 15, 1783,[10] and the Definitive Peace Treaty was ratified by Congress, convened in Annapolis, on January 13, 1784.[11] Congress issued a proclamation notifying the states of the treaty and ratification, "and requiring their observance thereof."[12] No states ratified, nor did any states ratify any of the treaties negotiated by the Congress under the Articles of Confederation.

The Preliminary Treaty of 1782 with Great Britain speaks in its preamble of an agreement between Richard Oswald, "the Commissioner of his Britannick Majesty for treating of peace with the commissioners of the United States of America," while article 1 is an acknowledgment by His Britannic Majesty of "the said United States," followed by a listing of the 13 states, declared "to be free, sovereign and independent States." The treaty mixes up singular and plural, a characteristic confusion which appears in all early treaties with the United States. Thus, the treaty describes "their Boundaries," whereas article 3 recognizes "that the people of the United States shall continue to enjoy" the "unmolested" right to fish on the Grand Bank and other locations. Article 5 explicitly reveals that it is with Congress that the Treaty is being made. Article 7 suggests that the British government recognized the citizens of the separate states, while article 8 speaks of "the Citizens of the United States."[13]

The Definitive Treaty of Peace that the three American commissioners negotiated with David Hartley carries a distinctive preamble in which the "King of Great Britain" reveals a desire "to forget all past Misunderstandings and Differences" with "the United States of America." The phraseology otherwise is identical, with references both to citizens of states and to citizens of the United States of America. The only material difference between the preliminary and definitive texts is that the latter provides for an exchange of ratification within six months from the day of the signing and, of course, omits the separate secret article about Florida.

It is my considered opinion that the treaties with France and Great Britain were made with the United States collectively and not with the individual states. I base this opinion on the unchallenged right of the Congress to conduct foreign relations even before the adoption of the Articles of Confederation. That authority was asserted as far back as November 29, 1775, when Congress appointed a five-man Committee of Correspondence to communicate with the European powers, and again on September 26, 1776, when Congress appointed a committee to prepare plans for treaties of commerce with foreign nations. From 1776 onward, without exception, American diplomatic commissions and the treaties negotiated under them contained such unequivocal terms as "the two parties," "the said two nations," "the two states," "the two republics," "of either nation," and "both nations."[14] As Mr. Justice Chase declared in *Ware* v. *Hylton,* "Congress properly possessed the great rights of external sovereignty: among others, the right to make treaties of commerce and alliance; as with France, on the 6th of February, 1778."[15]

It was Congress that appointed diplomatic representatives abroad and issued instructions and commissions in the name of the United States.[16] Acting under such a commission, John Jay was instructed to procure a treaty between Spain and "the citizens of the United States."[17] Speaking of his commission to the United Provinces, John Adams wrote the President of Congress, May 7, 1781, that he had "lately received from my sovereign, the United States of America in Congress assembled, a commission, with full powers and instructions to treat with the States-General concerning a treaty of amity and commerce."[18]

Just as the American diplomats commissioned by Congress to serve abroad acted under the authority of the United States in Congress Assembled, so, too, the commissioners named by Congress to negotiate peace with Great Britain carried commissions from the Congress, not from the States.[19] It was the United States in Congress Assembled that issued the instructions to the American peace commissioners.[20]

Not only were the American peace commissioners acting under election and by instructions of the United States in Congress Assembled, but their negotiations were carried on in behalf of the United States, not of the 13 states as separate entities. A brief review of the facts surrounding the peace negotiations between 1780 and 1782 should make this clear. During the

The Treaty of Paris of 1783

course of 1780 Austria and Russia, acting as comediators of the American War for Independence, each sponsored a proposal to negotiate with the 13 separate states rather than the Congress. Count Panin, the Russian chancellor, proposed a general armistice, during which period the king of France could require *each* of the 13 states to declare its intention and would thereafter only be obliged to maintain the independence of those states that wished to keep it.[21] The comte de Vergennes, France's foreign minister, expressed interest.[22] Such a proposal would, in his opinion, cut "the Gordian knot of the present war." Vergennes anticipated that a separate polling, colony by colony, as Panin advised, would then have resulted in partition. Panin implemented his suggested with a proposal for the holding of a peace congress, preferably at Leipzig, to which each of the "united colonies of America" would send delegates who would be accountable to their respective assemblies and not to Congress. That federal body, under Panin's plan, would remain suspended until each province had ruled on its own fate.[23] In turn, the Empress Catherine II suggested to the British ambassador, Sir James Harris, that England deal with the colonies separately. "Try to divide them. . . . That will provide a loop-hole for them, because one must realize that each power wishes to save his honor."[24]

In 1781, Prince von Kaunitz, the Austrian chancellor, likewise took up the proposal, urging that each of the 13 states send a deputy to treat separately with England.[25] Vergennes instructed his ambassador to Vienna to follow up this proposal, keeping in mind Panin's ingenious notion of separate consultations with each of the 13 states.[26] Should the emperor propose Panin's idea of having each state polled for its opinion of the peace, "let us act surprised," he instructed his ambassador at St. Petersburg in March 1781.[27] Several weeks later he asked Vérac, the French envoy, to ascertain from Panin the basis upon which he was preparing to admit the American delegates to the congress.[28]

At the same time Prince von Kaunitz raised with Breteuil, France's ambassador to Vienna, the possibility of having each state send a deputy to the congress to treat separately of its affairs with England and in that way to secure England's consent to their representation.[29] Breteuil wrote Vergennes, objecting to the plan and pointing out that a considerable number of deputies would give Britain the opportunity of fomenting disunion and discord among the United States.[30] Instead, Vergennes pounced on the proposal and asked Breteuil to follow up the lead, suggesting that the deputies might be chosen by their separate assemblies.[31]

John Adams, minister plenipotentiary, appointed by Congress in the fall of 1779 to negotiate and conclude a peace with Great Britain, along with a treaty of commerce, clarified the legal and constitutional issues for the comte de Vergennes in a conference during the first week of July 1781, held to discuss the prospects of a comediation by Emperor Joseph II and Empress Catherine II. Adams pointed out to Vergennes that the United States could not be represented in a congress of European powers without recognition of their independence and served notice that the proposal then mooted of carrying on separate consultations with each of the 13 states was entirely unacceptable. He reminded Vergennes that the Articles of Confederation had been ratified and communicated to the courts of Europe and were as "universally known as any constitution of government in Europe," that the American Constitution expressly delegated to the United States in Congress Assembled the power and authority to negotiate with foreign powers, and that for any power to apply to the governors or legislatures of the separate states would be "a public disrespect." It would be an error and a misdemeanor for a state official to receive and transmit such a communication to his respective legislature. In short, there was "no method for the courts of Europe to convey anything to the people of America but through the Congress of the United States, nor any way of negotiating with them but by means of that body." With these constitutional obstructions in mind, Adams strongly urged Vergennes to discountenance the notion of "summoning ministers from the Thirteen States."[32]

That ended France's interest in the proposal. Henceforth, it was clear to all the negotiating powers that negotiations were being conducted with a single nation, the United States of America.

Significantly, the Treaty of Paris of 1783 recognizes United States citizenship. Did such exist in the year 1783? There is no question about the existence of state citizenship, which was a carryover from citizenship in the separate colonies. But that United States citizenship had been conferred in the years of the American Revolution seems clear from correspondence between John Jay, while he was minister plenipotentiary to Spain, and Benjamin Franklin, the American commissioner to Paris. In 1781 John Vaughan, brother of Benjamin, the celebrated intermediary between Shelburne and Jay, arrived in Madrid and consulted Jay about embarking for America and settling in Philadelphia. Could not Jay administer to him the oath of United States citizenship, he asked. Since Jay, a prudent lawyer, strictly construed the powers granted him under his commission from Congress, he turned to Franklin, the senior diplomat abroad. Franklin answered: "My brother ministers here, I believe, considered themselves as vested with consular powers, and to be therefore capable of administering an oath, and I have continued the practice conceiving them to be better lawyers than myself." Thus, while expressing a desire for some explicit instructions from Congress on the question, he seems to have administered oaths of United States citizenship and issued passports.[33]

From the variety of evidential data, along with the text of the Treaty of 1783 itself, there can be no doubt, then, that the treaty was made with the United States of America in Congress Assembled and not with the individual states as principals. As Thomas Paine put it succinctly in the 13th *American Crisis* paper (April 19, 1783), "We have no other national sovereignty than as United States."

Much has been made of the geographical misconceptions which prevailed at the peacemaking because of the reliance upon the celebrated Mitchell map. Only recently I visited the Newberry Library, where Dr. Lester Cappon, John H. Long, and other able staff members are engaged in demonstrating the serious geographical distortions, both areal as well as linear, which the map embodied.[34] Relying largely on this map, the negotiators accepted as a northeastern boundary the mysterious "St. Croix River," which in fact proved to be two rivers, and assumed that the source of the Mississippi was to be found in Canada. Hence, the strange provision of article 8 of the Definitive Treaty that "the navigation of the River Mississippi, from its source to the ocean shall for ever remain free and open to the subjects of Great Britain and the citizens of the United States." That both the northeastern and the northwestern boundaries were the subject of later renegotiation is a commonplace in American history.

What is relevant at this very moment, however, is that portion of article 2 of the Definitive Treaty which, after tracing the northeastern boundary, adds the significant phrase:

. . . comprehending all Islands within twenty Leagues of any Part of the Shores of the United States, and lying between Lines to be drawn due East from the Points where the aforesaid Boundaries between Nova Scotia on the one Part and East Florida on the other, shall respectively touch the Bay of Fundy and the Atlantic Ocean, excepting such Islands as now are or heretofore have been within the limits of the said province of Nova Scotia.

It is the contention of the Common Council Atlantic States in the current litigation of *U.S.* v. *Maine et al.* that, along with vague claims resting upon provisions in some of the ancient charters, like that of Virginia of 1609, the wording in article 2 represents a seaward boundary of the United States given to the individual states individually rather than collectively and supports the claims of those states to offshore drilling rights on the continental shelf of the Atlantic coast. The federal government denies that either the states or the federal government ever held a property in the seabed or subsoil of the Atlantic coast beyond low water mark, contending that the three-mile limit advanced by Jefferson as Secretary of State was merely an assertion of sovereignty for defensive purposes and not a claim of title and that all rights to the seabed and subsoil off the coast vest in the United States as a result of President Truman's Proclamation of 1945 and subsequent international agreements.[35] That view was upheld in all subsequent litigation beginning with *U.S. v. California* in 1947.[36]

Granted that the issue is of momentous consequence in view of the energy crisis facing this country and our reliance upon energy sources now provided us by nations whose future relations are at best unpredictable, what concerns us as historians is the relevance of the evidence from the peacemaking of 1782–83 to this issue. At least two maps were drawn up in the course of the preliminary negotiations. The so-called "King George's Map," now in the custody of the British Museum, has the discussed boundaries in negotiation superimposed upon a copy of the Mitchell map, with a red line running between Nova Scotia and Massachusetts (Maine, of course, after 1820) and then continuing down along the Atlantic coast. The red line bears the annotation "Boundary as described by Mr. Oswald." The annotation appears twice along the line in the Atlantic "comprehending all Islands within Twenty Leagues of . . . the Shore of the United States." Other annotated lines on this map designate—incorrectly—the lines of the Treaty of Utrecht according to British and French construction. The latter treaty gave the British fishing rights within 30 leagues of the fishing banks, but these rights did not extend down the Atlantic coast.[37]

Similarly, the copy John Jay used during the preliminary negotiations, now owned by the New-York Historical Society, also carries a line about 20 leagues off the coast from Florida to Maine which bears the legend "Mr. Oswald's Line" in Jay's handwriting. The line on the map is the tentative line of October 8, 1783, provisionally agreed upon with Richard Oswald, the British commissioner.

Neither map, nor any of the others subsequently located in connection with the Maine–New Brunswick boundary negotiations, can be accepted as authentic evidence of the intent of the peace commissioners as regards the description contained in the Definitive Treaty.[38]

Aside from their lack of official standing, the lines drawn on the King George's and Jay maps continuing from the northeastern boundary and running 20 leagues off the coast to Florida are not a seaward boundary line of the United States but a delineation, in accordance with the instructions of the American commissioners and the terms of the Preliminary and

Definitive Treaties, of islands awarded the United States which fell inside the 20-league area. Significantly, the American commissioners followed their instructions from Congress to the letter in this regard. The ultimatum of Congress of August 4, 1779, included the phrase "comprehending all islands within twenty leagues of any part of the shores of the United States, between lines drawn due east from the points where their boundary lines between Nova Scotia on the one part and Florida on the other part shall touch the Atlantic Ocean," virtually the same wording as the final treaty, excepting in the latter case such islands deemed to be within the limits of Nova Scotia.[39]

These maps drawn up during the preliminaries are dubious evidence at best and clearly have no legal standing. The final, formal, signed copies of both the Preliminary and Definitive Treaties bearing the attested signatures of the British and American commissioners and submitted both to Congress and to the government of Great Britain for ratification contained no maps, nor did they have any maps attached thereto. What was approved, and what was ratified, was a handwritten text of the treaties unaccompanied by maps, drawings, diagrams, or illustrations in any form. What governs is the text. That only islands were comprehended by the line, not seabed or subsoil, is self-evident from the text itself.

Furthermore, the 20-league line by no means served to confine the activities of the United States or of American citizens. It is clear from article 3 of the Definitive Treaty, giving to the "people of the United States unmolested" the right to fish on the Grand Bank and on all other banks of Newfoundland, that the United States gained rights considerably eastward of the 20-league line. Thus, the fishing banks, extending from George's Bank on the southwest to Flemish Cap on the east, stretch a distance of 1,100 miles and with a varying width of 50 to 250 miles.[40] In this area the right of the people of the United States to fish was recognized by the Treaty of 1783, and, significantly, this area falls largely to the east of the 20-league line marked on the map.

It is also significant that, except for the working-paper maps used in the course of the preliminary negotiations, maps depicting the new United States published after 1782 and incorporating the results of the Preliminary and Definitive Treaties of Peace of 1782 and 1783 do not reproduce the line shown on the King George's map. The first map of the United States to be created in the United States after the peace was the Abel Buell map, "A New and Correct Map of the United States of North America" (1784), and that map fails to indicate such a line. Nor does one of the earliest globes produced around this time, Cary's Terrestrial Globe. Other maps of the period immediately after 1783 which have been examined similarly fail to include such a line, although in some cases the fishing banks are designated.[41]

From the abundant evidence cited it seems perfectly clear that neither the King George's copy nor the Jay copy of the Mitchell map represents a seaward boundary of the United States save as comprehending offshore islands in the Atlantic Ocean acquired by the United States under the Treaty of Paris in 1783.

It may be added that the controversy over the impressment of seamen in the early national period makes it abundantly clear that the United States contested the right of Great Britain to impress seamen, not only in United States territorial waters but on the high seas as well, and even went so far as to deny Britain's historic offshore claims around her own islands. This amounted to an implicit denial of the claims of either the United States or Great Britain to exercising sovereign rights outside its own territorial waters narrowly defined. It is also clear that Great Britain, a cosigner of the Definitive Treaty of 1783, did not regard the waters within the 20-league line as an area in which American ships were exempt from search and seizure in peacetime and clearly implied by her actions that she did not deem the 20-league line to have fixed an eastern boundary for the territories of the United States.[42]

To the editor of the Papers of John Jay it is perhaps more than fortuitous that all of the issues which were presumably settled with Great Britain by the Peace of 1783, but were in fact unsettled, along with the vital issue of the navigation of the Mississippi about which Spain had remained obdurate during the course of the American Revolution, remained to be dealt with by the principal negotiator of the Treaty of 1783, John Jay, whether as Secretary for Foreign Affairs in the Confederation years, as Chief Justice of the United States Supreme Court, or as minister plenipotentiary to Great Britain. Fate seemed to have placed all the cards in Jay's own hand, but when he sought clarification of all these vital issues during his secretaryship he could hardly have reckoned upon the depth of sectional feeling, the powerful debtor lobby, the coming of the French Revolution, the rise of the two-party system, or the duplicity of his associate Alexander Hamilton.

None of these issues in the great drama of implementing the provisions of the treaty with Great Britain, of securing the long-sought-after commercial treaty with the mother country, or of gaining for American citizens free access to the Gulf of Mexico could be settled in camera or by unilateral action on the part of a very weak United States. How Jay handled each of these issues in turn will probably remain a subject of controversy to the end of time. As Secretary for Foreign Affairs he attempted, perhaps halfheartedly, to work out a compromise with Spain on the issue of the Mississippi, a compromise which, incidentally, so strong a nationalist as the Virginian George Washington approved. Failing to secure ratification of the agreement from Congress, Jay bided his time. Obviously the concessions he made to the British in the treaty of 1794 that bears his name seemed so portentous to the Spaniards that Pinckney had little trouble securing concessions from Spain that Jay himself could not obtain by direct negotiations with Don Diego de Gardoqui.[43] Would it be straining the evidence to analogize between these two successive treaties and the remarkable impact that the detente between the People's Republic of China and the United States has had in bringing about a speedy settlement of a whole series of issues long outstanding between the Soviet Union and America?

It was John Adams, not Franklin or Jay, who insisted on placing no impediment in the way of the collection of debts due British and Loyalist creditors, but it was Jay who drafted the article as it appears in the treaty. Article 4 reads: "It is agreed that creditors on either side shall meet with no lawful impediment to the recovery of the full value in sterling money of all bona fide debts heretofore contracted." More than any single man, it was Jay who was to see that this clause was carried out to the letter. Jay never for a moment forgot his role in the drafting of this provision. As the first Chief Justice he upheld the validity of prewar debts guaranteed by the treaty to which his signature was affixed. Thus, when in 1785 John Adams called upon the British government to evacuate the frontier posts which they held in violation of the Treaty of Paris, the Marquess of Carmarthen, the British foreign minister, refused to give them up on the ground that the United States had failed to remove the legal impediments in the way of recovery of debts.

This issue of who broke the treaty first has a contemporary ring, sounded in post-armistice disputes between the United States on the one side and North Vietnam and the Vietcong, both as regards the supplying of arms inside South Vietnam and the responsibility for the current tragic flareup in Cambodia. Surprisingly, Jay recognized the obduracy of the state legislatures and courts in the matter of the debts, and it only stiffened a very stiff backbone. In a long report on Carmarthen's note, submitted to Congress in secret session in October 1786, Jay declared that Great Britain was justified in retaining the posts. One could not blame her for holding onto them, he argued, while the United States on its side impeded full execution of the treaty. Curiously, as Samuel Flagg Bemis has pointed out, Jay felt obliged to divulge in confidence the nature of his report to Sir

John Temple, the British consul at New York.

Bowing to Jay's demands, Congress passed a resolution calling upon the states to remove such obstacles and submitting a copy thereof to each state. Accompanying the congressional resolution was a circular letter composed by Jay, wherein he pointed out the impolicy and bad faith inhering in a failure to execute treaty engagements "constitutionally and fairly made" by the Confederation, as well as the inconvenience and absurdity of subjecting their terms to the varying interpretations of the legislatures of the 13 separate states.[44]

As we know, the resolution of Congress was honored in the breach, notably by the state of Virginia. Even James Madison, a model of probity, wrote Jefferson just before Virginia ratified the Constitution that the only opposition he foresaw to the adoption of the Constitution by his state might come from "ill-timed or rigorous execution of the Treaty of Peace against British debtors."[45] Mr. Madison's Constitution prohibited the states from passing any law impairing the obligation of contracts (art. 1, sect. 10), gave the federal courts jurisdiction over all cases arising from the treaties made under the authority of the United States (art. 3, sect. 2), and declared such treaties to be the supreme law of the land (art. 6).

As Chief Justice, Jay relished the opportunity of reminding federal grand juries of the sanctity of treaties. Even as late as the May term of 1793, Jay, hardly by coincidence, adverted to the subject of treaty obligations in a charge to the grand jury at Richmond. Though exposed to abuse, he managed to avoid assassination, which surely some of the debtors must have considered too good a fate for him.[46] Immediately after Jay's charge to the grand jury, he sat in the case of *Ware* v. *Hylton,* which involved a suit by British creditors. By a split decision judgment was given in favor of the British creditors, and the exception as regards sums which debtors had paid into the State Treasury was overruled on appeal.[47]

Despite affirmative decisions in federal and state courts, the issue remained unresolved, first, because the federal courts had no jurisdiction over debts under $500 and, second, because the debtors, although reconciled to paying the principal, resisted paying the interest on the sums due. Dispatched by Washington on a mission to England to resolve this and other unsettled treaty issues, Jay inserted in the final treaty a clause providing for appeals from the American courts on the creditor issue to a mixed commission to decide on these claims, which the United States was to pay in specie. Thus, Jay made it possible for British claimants to circumvent the American courts and utilize a procedure which would expedite their claims while failing to secure a comparable provision concerning American claimants. The latter were required to run the gamut of the British judicial system before a mixed commission sitting in London would entertain their suits.

Admittedly, the debt provisions of the treaty are less than evenhanded, and one wonders why the Chief Justice stripped his own court of jurisdiction over cases which it had shown itself competent to rule upon with impartiality. On the credit side, praise is due Jay for removing from the Court a very sensitive political issue which could not possibly enhance its national prestige, and at the same time for his notable innovation in international law, the principle of mixed commissions, which the United States and Great Britain subsequently used in the settlement of their disputes. Jay had drawn the notion from his service when a young attorney as secretary of the New York–New Jersey Boundary Commission. With that colonial experience in mind, Jay provided in his treaty for the appointment of a joint commission to hear claims arising under the treaty of 1783; two of its members were to be named by the United States and two by Great Britain, and a fifth member was to be selected by the appointed commissioners. As it worked out the four commissioners selected the fifth member by lot, and the choice fell upon the British nominee, giving the British a majority on the commission, with an ensuing deadlock, which Jefferson settled by a compromise formula under the Convention of 1802. In this convention the United States agreed to pay £600,000 sterling to the British government in settlement of all outstanding claims, an amount that was duly paid from the treasury of the United States in three annual installments. With interest added, the claimant creditors obtained over 46 percent of the amounts validated by a British domestic commission.[48]

The peace negotiations of the American Revolution suggest all sorts of tantalizing analogies to the recent past and the troubled present. We may, if we choose, find striking parallels between the negotiations of 1782–83 involving the Great Powers and the American insurgents and the long protracted parleys some years back between the French government and the Algerian rebels. The American commissioners, it must be remembered, sought not only independence but territorial integrity and elbow room. We might compare their insistence upon the inclusion of the trans-Appalachian West with demands pressed by the Algerian nationalists to the French Sahara. America's claims were perhaps stronger, although its strength lay in its claims as successor to the Crown of Great Britain's cessions obtained by the Peace of 1763 rather than upon the less tenable clauses of ancient charters with their extravagant coast-to-coast grants that nobody, least of all the British government, was taking seriously before 1776. Having repudiated the British Crown, the states were scarcely in a powerful juridical or moral position to assert the Crown's claims and title. Furthermore, these claims, like the Algerian, were not bolstered by effective military occupation. It must be borne in mind that the bulk of the territory George Rogers Clark had conquered in the Northwest had largely slipped from America's grip by the close of the war. Those short-lived conquests cut little ice in the actual peace negotiations. All the Great Powers opposed America's winning of the West, and indubitably the claims of both Spain and England to that region were strong ones. But after a partition of the American continent, desired by everyone but America, the new republic would not have been left with a durable fragment. Similarly, the partition of Algeria according to the myriad plans that were put forth, would not have assured the FLN a viable state, nor would the secession of Katanga or Oriente provinces have allowed the Congo the wherewithal to survive and prosper.

The Algerian negotiations suggest a still further analogy to the American Revolutionary settlement. In both sets of negotiations, the loyalists, or refugees, as in all future negotiations with Castro's Cuba, posed a thorny problem. Both with Algeria and America the rights and grievances of this substantial segment of the population loyal to the mother country, or in the case of Cuba opposed to the Castro regime, threatened to prevent any agreement from being carried out. In the case of Cuba the issue of the refugees mounts a formidable obstacle to negotiations with the United States. Neither the American nor the Algerian settlements effectively protected the loyalists in fact, and both were followed by mass loyalist emigrations.

Even more tantalizing is the analogy between King George III's obstinate course in refusing to recognize the insurgent Americans who held part but not all of the 13 states, and the long years in which the United States refused to deal directly with the Vietcong, who still hold part but by no means all of South Vietnam.

In our own time it seems to be uncritically accepted that the people, as distinguished from their governments, are peace loving, while the government leaders are the warmongers. This is in fact a gross oversimplification. Often as not the public is not prepared for a peace involving the abandonment of most war aims because it lacks all the facts and perhaps has always lacked them. One might indeed analogize the Vietnamese conflict with the American Revolution. Both were long-drawn-out wars, and both sides were weary of war. That was truly the case by the summer of 1780. At that time one side was perhaps more hard pressed than the other, but the British, rebounding from a series of defeats by the capture of Charleston, were by

The Treaty of Paris of 1783

no manner of means hanging over the ropes. Even after Yorktown a case could be made that the War of the Revolution in its world phase had come to a deadlock. The British had been clearly defeated in America, although their army of at least 10,000 men was quite capable of starting some trouble anew. On the other hand, the British had proved quite successful in Europe in repulsing their foes, and extraordinarily successful in India and the East Indies.

It would be rash to assume that the British public was prepared for heavy sacrifices. Shelburne's correspondents, during the summer of 1782, contributed to his wavering further in his readiness to concede unconditional independence by demanding that he hold out and not yield that crucial point to the Americans. This helps explain his ambivalence on that issue— the double words he used in Parliament as contrasted with the private reassurances he was sending on to the Americans either through his peace commissioner or through an intermediary.

But if the public was not prepared for the sacrifices which peace entails, neither was the leadership. The obduracy of George III on the score of conceding final and irrevocable independence to the Americans is too notorious for documentation, while Charles III of Spain was psychologically unready to accept defeat at Gibraltar and kept insisting on recovering a fortress that he and his ally had signally failed to recapture.

To an extent, then, peace was brought about by a deception both of the public and of the kingly rulers. How George III took the provisional treaty we know from his lugubrious and maladroit appearance before Parliament hardly a week after the preliminaries had been signed. It is significant that the parliamentary debate over the announcement of American independence broke out long before the preliminary treaties with France, Spain, and America were laid upon the table for the inspection of the members, which was on January 27, 1783, almost two months after the American preliminaries. Still, they were neither circularized nor printed. Much consternation and a good deal of ridicule ensued when the Lords went ahead and printed the treaties before the Commons did.

Now, I am not suggesting that either the public or the Senate of the United States would tolerate such secret diplomacy today, but there were moments when it was touch-and-go, and when an outraged monarch, a suspicious Parliament, and an unenlightened public, either in combination or singly, would have been sufficient to tip the balance against peace.

Nowhere is this better illustrated than in the secret negotiations conducted by French Undersecretary Gerard de Rayneval in London and Bowood in behalf of Spain. Shelburne and George III, who panted after a rich sugar island, were prepared to make a deal on Gibraltar, but when news leaked out that the leaders were willing to yield the fortress that had been so gloriously and successfully defended, public opinion, as understood in those days, was thoroughly aroused. Now Shelburne could not get enough votes in his cabinet to support a trade involving Gibraltar. Richmond blew up and Keppel threatened that both he and the duke would resign if the ministry did not cling to Gibraltar. That was enough for the king, who was tired of acrimony.

Vergennes, who wished to remain master of the negotiations for the Spaniards if he had already lost control in effect over the Americans, now let it be known that he would engage his country to induce the Spaniards to abandon their demands for Gibraltar. The alternatives Vergennes now proposed were thoroughly unacceptable to a mutinous British Cabinet that proved much more intransigent on this point than had either George III or Shelburne; and Rayneval, the French undersecretary of foreign affairs, realizing that the tide had turned, informed the British that he would accept for Spain the Floridas and Minorca as equivalents for Gibraltar. Neither the undersecretary nor his chief, the comte de Vergennes, would hold up the war for Gibraltar a moment longer, and they so informed the conde de Aranda, Spain's plenipotentiary at Versailles. Aranda saw the light, and on his own responsibility, and in defiance of explicit instructions to the contrary, he bowed to the French—and it was then too late for an angry Spanish monarch and an infuriated Spanish principal minister to repudiate their own envoy. As a result Gibraltar is still British, although every so often the battle seems to be renewed, and the stakes on either side now seem so inconsequential that the issue evokes merely a diplomatic yawn on the part of the powers not directly concerned.

Despite Woodrow Wilson's pledge for "open covenants openly arrived at," one would be quite innocent to suggest that secret diplomacy has vanished in our time. However, peace commissioners, as even Henry Kissinger learned, are no longer given plenipotentiary and binding powers. The heads of state reserve the right to repudiate them. The peace envoys are under telephone and Telex barrage from the head man back home, and when the final showdown nears one can be certain that a Secretary of State or a President will appear on the scene to complete the deal.

The American peacemakers capitalized on the factors of time and distance to keep the initiative and even to ignore humiliating instructions which they felt were contrary to the national interest; and even the conde de Aranda, who doubtless wanted to settle some old scores with his political foe the conde de Floridablanca, presented a heroic figure in standing out against his king and ministry. "Respect and obedience bound me to blind submission," Aranda defended himself, "but the loyalty of a good subject and an awareness of the real situation compelled me to do what was right." Today instant communication has invalidated the grounds for conferring plenipotentiary powers on peace negotiators, but it has not eliminated the need for cool judgment and courage, the willingness of the ultimate peacemakers to accept the acceptable, to weigh the national interest against the felt needs of the human race rather than to quake at the clamor of a short-sighted, nationalist-oriented segment of the public. While such a course demands courage, to be sure, it must be borne in mind, as the truce settlement in Vietnam has shown, that the instruments for shaping public opinion in the hands of a state were never so potent as at the present time. I might add that making peace is one matter, going to war or engaging in hostilities which amount in fact to war but avoid that dreaded terminology, another. As regards the latter, the constitutional safeguards inhibiting hasty, impulsive, or even secret decisions must once more be observed, since the declaration of war is a power conferred by the Constitution upon the Congress.

The negotiations conducted with the American commissioners at Paris in 1783 disclosed how obdurate a revolutionary state can be when vital issues are at stake. If I may be permitted a quotation from a closing paragraph of *The Peacemakers* by way of summary:

> True, the Peace of Paris and Versailles of 1783 was no *diktat* forced upon a conquered people, but rather a negotiated peace with an adversary who had managed, aside from North America, to avoid humiliating defeat. Such a peace involved concessions on both sides. What was so remarkable about the achievements of the American commissioners was that where they compromised it was on inessentials and where they conceded it was to yield the trivial. From beginning to end they remained unswerving on the score of obtaining both absolute independence and a continental domain for thirteen littoral states. On the main objectives of national survival they proved uncompromising. Because the American commissioners resolutely contended for the right of a sovereign people to choose their own form of government and because they secured grudging recognition of that right from the Old Order, a free people is eternally in their debt.[49]

Notes

[1] Treaty ser., no. 104, in U.S. Treaties, etc., *Treaties and Other International Acts of the United States of America, 1776–1863,* ed. David Hunter Miller, 8 vols. (Washington: U.S. Govt. Print. Off., 1931–48), 2:151–56.

[2] Richard B. Morris, *The Peacemakers; the Great Powers and American Independence* (New York: Harper & Row, 1965).

[3] Henri Doniol, *Histoire de la Participation de la France à l'établissement des États-Unis d'Amérique,* 5 vols. (Paris: Imprimerie nationale, 1886–92), 3:803–10.

[4] Don Juan de Miralles to José de Galvez, December 28, 1778, Archivo General de Indias, Seville, Ind. Ger. 1606.

[5] For the congressional debates and instructions regarding peace objectives, insofar as they affected Britain on the one hand and France and Spain on the other, see Morris, *The Peacemakers,* esp. chaps. 1 and 11. See also Transcript of Testimony of Richard B. Morris in *U.S. v. State of Maine et al.,* Supreme Court of the United States, Autumn Term 1972, No. 35, Original.

[6] See U.S. Continental Congress, *Journals of the Continental Congress, 1774–1789,* ed. Worthington C. Ford et al., 34 vols. (Washington: Library of Congress, 1904–37), 14:958–59 (August 14, 1779), and for earlier references, ibid., 10:379 and 11:615, 701.

[7] U.S. Treaties, etc., *Treaties, Conventions, International Acts, Protocols, and Agreements Between the United States of America and Other Powers,* comp. William M. Malloy, 4 vols. (Washington: U.S. Govt. Print. Off., 1910–38).

[8] James Brown Scott, *Sovereign States and Suits Before Arbitral Tribunals and Courts of Justice* (New York: New York University Press, 1925), pp. 55–57; also pp. 35–40, 46–47, 54, 63.

[9] Thomas Jefferson, *The Papers of Thomas Jefferson,* ed. Julian P. Boyd (Princeton: Princeton University Press, 1950–), 9:264.

[10] *Journals of the Continental Congress,* 24:241–43.

[11] Edmund C. Burnett, ed., *Letters of Members of the Continental Congress,* 8 vols. (Washington: Carnegie Institution of Washington, 1921–36), 7:410–14.

[12] *Journals of the Continental Congress,* 26:29.

[13] For the preliminary text, see Samuel Flagg Bemis, *The Diplomacy of the American Revolution* (Bloomington: Indiana University Press, 1957), pp. 259–64.

[14] See, for example, the French Treaty of Amity and Commerce, *Journals of the Continental Congress,* 11:421; proposed Dutch treaty, November 1779, ibid., 15:1235; final Dutch treaty, January 23, 1783, ibid., 24:68, 75, 80; treaty with Sweden, July 29, 1783, ibid., 24:458, 468, 470.

[15] 3 Dallas 199 (1796).

[16] See *Journals of the Continental Congress,* 8:520 (July 1, 1777); 11:546, 547 (May 28, 1778); 15:1121 (September 28, 1779); 18:1168–71 (December 1780).

[17] Ibid., 15:1121 (September 28, 1779).

[18] U.S. Dept. of State, *The Revolutionary Diplomatic Correspondence of the United States*, ed. Francis Wharton, 6 vols. (Washington: Govt. Print. Off., 1889), 6:402.

[19] *Journals of the Continental Congress*, 20:652–54.

[20] See *Journals of the Continental Congress*, 14:920 (August 4, 1779); 16:116, 117 (September 28, 1779); 20:615–17, 651–52, 713–14 (June 1781).

[21] Marquis de Vérac to comte de Vergennes, September 1, 1780, Correspondance politique, Ministère des affaires étrangères (Paris), Russie, 105:96, 337–46.

[22] Vergennes to Vérac, two letters, October 8, 1780, and again in a despatch of October 12, 1780, Correspondance politique, Russie, 105:241, 243, 368, 369.

[23] Vérac to Vergennes, November 14, 1780, Correspondance politique, Russie, 105:324–31.

[24] James Harris, 1st Earl of Malmesbury, *Diaries and Correspondence of James Harris, first Earl of Malmesbury . . . Edited by his grandson, the third Earl*, 4 vols. (London: R. Bentley, 1844; reprint ed., New York: AMS Press, 1970), 1:357.

[25] Vérac to Vergennes, February 18/March 1, 1781, Correspondance politique, Russie, 106:156–63; Baron de Breteuil to Vergennes, February 11, 1781, Correspondance politique, Autriche, 342:56.

[26] Vergennes to Breteuil, March 4, 1781, Correspondance politique, Autriche, 342:92.

[27] Vergennes to Vérac, March 11, 1781, Correspondance politique, Russie, 106:177–79.

[28] Vergennes to Vérac, April 7, 1781, Correspondance politique, Russie, 106:229–32.

[29] Breteuil to Vergennes, April 19, 1781, Correspondance politique, Autriche, 342:237.

[30] Ibid.

[31] Vergennes to Breteuil, May 7, 1781, Correspondance politique, Autriche, 342:300.

[32] John Adams to Vergennes, July 21, 1781, Correspondance politique, États-Unis, 17:441; Wharton, *Revolutionary Diplomatic Correspondence*, 4:595–96.

[33] John Jay to Benjamin Franklin, Aranjuez, May 31, 1781; Franklin to Jay, Passy, August 20, 1781, Franklin Papers, 5:156–60, 6:21–22, Library of Congress.

[34] For the use of the Mitchell map by the peace negotiators, see Wharton, *Revolutionary Diplomatic Correspondence*, 6:131–33; Franklin, John Adams, Jay, and Laurens to Robert R. Livingston, December 14, 1782 (although other maps were also consulted according to Adams and Jay); testimony of John Adams, August 15, 1797, in the St. Croix River arbitration, in John Bassett Moore, ed., *International Adjudications, Ancient and Modern* . . . (New York: Oxford University Press, 1929–), Modern Series, 1:63; and deposition of John Jay, May 21, 1798, ibid., 1:65.

[35] By the Submerged Lands Act, Congress in 1953 gave to California those rights in the marginal sea and seabed to the three-mile limit. 43 U.S.C. §§1301 *et seq.* (1964).

[36] 332 U.S. 19 (1947).

[37] Fred L. Israel, ed., *Major Peace Treaties of Modern History, 1648–1967*, 4 vols. (New York: Chelsea House Publishers, 1967), 1:209.

[38] See Hunter Miller, *Treaties and Other International Acts of the United States*, 3:349.

[39] *Journals of the Continental Congress*, 14:920, 921. For the slight modification of the instructions to John Adams 10 days later, see ibid., 14:958 (August 14, 1779).

[40] See Raymond McFarland, *A History of the New England Fisheries* (Philadelphia: University of Pennsylvania; New York: D. Appleton and Company, agents, 1911), p. 6.

[41] In addition to the Buell map, the maps examined include: "A New Map of North America, with the West Indies, Divided According to the Preliminary Articles of Peace, signed at Versailles, 20 January 1783," reproduced in Thomas Jefferys et al., *The American Atlas: or, A Geographical Description of the Whole Continent of America* (1794); "A New and Correct Map of North America, with the West India Islands, Divided According to the last Treaty of Paris, concluded at Paris the 20th of January 1783," engraved and published by Matthew Albert and George Frederic Lotter, 1784; Samuel Dunn, "A New Map of the United States of North America, with the British Dominions on that Continent, etc.," 1786; "North America Drawn from the Latest and Best Authorities," 1787; and Thomas Kitchin, "North America, wherein are particularly distinguished the British Dominions, the United States, and the Adjacent Spanish Territories," 1794, reproduced in Thomas Jefferys et al., *The American Atlas* (London, 1794).

[42] For the relevance of the impressment issue to the definition of territorial limits, see S. F. Bemis, "The London Mission of Thomas Pinckney," *American Historical Review* (1913):240, quoting from Foreign Office papers; "Report of the Naturalization Commission of 1869," in Great Britain, *Reports from Commissioners: 1868-9* (London, 1869), 25:32-33, Appendix 1; U.S. Congress, *American State Papers, Documents, Legislative and Executive, of the Congress of the United States, Class I, Foreign Relations*, 6 vols. (Washington: Gales and Seaton, 1832-61), 2:493, 3:25-26, 85; Rufus King to Timothy Pickering, March 10, 1804, *The Life and Correspondence of Rufus King*, ed. Charles R. King, 6 vols. (New York: G. P. Putnam's Sons, 1894-1900), 4:368-69. See also James F. Zimmerman, *Impressment of American Seamen* (1925; reprint ed., Port Washington, N.Y.: Kennikat Press, 1966).

[43] See Samuel F. Bemis, *Pinckney's Treaty; America's Advantage from Europe's Distress, 1783-1800*, rev. ed. (New Haven: Yale University Press, 1960).

[44] *Journals of the Continental Congress*, 32:175-84 (April 13, 1787).

[45] James Madison, *The Writings of James Madison* . . . , ed. Gaillard Hunt, 9 vols. (New York: G. P. Putnam's Sons, 1900-10), 5:240-41.

[46] See Richard B. Morris, *John Jay, the Nation, and the Court* (Boston: Boston University Press, 1967), pp. 84-87.

[47] Ibid., pp. 88, 89; 3 Dallas 199-285.

[48] *American State Papers, Foreign Relations*, 2:382-428; H. Neufeld, *The International Protection of Private Creditors From the Treaties of Westphalia to the Congress of Vienna (1648-1815)* (Leiden: Sijthoff, 1971), pp. 77-78.

[49] Morris, *The Peacemakers*, p. 459.

RICHARD B. MORRIS began his teaching career in 1927 as an instructor in history at the City College of New York, where he taught for 22 years. He joined the Columbia University faculty in 1949, served as chairman of the History Department, 1959–61, and since 1959 has been the Gouverneur Morris Professor of History.

Professor Morris holds a B.A. degree from the City College of New York, M.A. and Ph.D. degrees from Columbia University, and an L.H.D. degree from Hebrew Union College. He has been a visiting professor and lecturer at many universities in the United States and abroad, including Princeton University, the University of Hawaii, and the Free University of Berlin. In 1961 he received an appointment as a Fulbright research scholar at the University of Paris.

Among Professor Morris' many publications are *Government and Labor in Early America* (1946), *The American Revolution, a Short History* (1955), *The Spirit of 'Seventy-Six* (with Henry S. Commager, 1958, 1967), *The Peacemakers; the Great Powers and American Independence* (1965), awarded the Bancroft Prize in history, *The American Revolution Reconsidered* (1967), *The Emerging Nations and the American Revolution* (1970), *America, a History of the People* (with William Greenleaf and Robert H. Ferrell, 1971), and most recently, *Seven Who Shaped Our Destiny: The Founding Fathers as Revolutionaries* (1973). Professor Morris is principal investigator of the papers of John Jay and is a member of the Advisory Committee on the Library of Congress American Revolution Bicentennial Program.

It is a sobering reflection—one that I think is particularly important for us to make at the present time—that with a few notable exceptions, such as John Adams and James Madison, these great testamentary documents were not the work of men trained in the academy. Jefferson "quitted college" after two years. Franklin had a grammar school education. Washington had almost no formal schooling. Roger Sherman was a cobbler. But, whatever their schooling, the leaders of that generation knew how to fabricate the fundamental documents on which rested a new and enduring kind of federal republic.

To discuss the meaning that these documents have for our own troubled time, we have with us James Russell Wiggins. Like Benjamin Franklin, he was unencumbered by college or university training. Also, like Franklin, he rose to eminence through almost half a century of experience as a professional journalist. He began with the Rock County Star, Luverne, Minn., *at the age of 19 and went on to the executive editorship and vice presidency of the* Washington Post, *one of the great newspapers of America. He is the author of* Freedom or Secrecy, *a brilliant and penetrating analysis of the role of the press in a free society. He is a past president of the American Society of Newspaper Editors. He is president of one of our oldest and finest learned societies, the American Antiquarian Society. After his retirement from the* Washington Post, *he entered upon his present career as editor and publisher of the* Ellsworth American. *Journalist, historian, and diplomat, Mr. Wiggins is also, like Thomas Jefferson, both exponent and champion of the press.*

The Fundamental Testaments Today

JAMES RUSSELL WIGGINS

THE UTTERANCES AND THE DOCUMENTS that have the most influence upon the events of an age are likely to be those which speak to the problems immediately at hand the most emphatically, the most dramatically, and the most persuasively. It is their timeliness and not their timelessness that makes them the effectual agents of reform or revolution. Their very pertinence to an existing situation often tends to diminish their relevance to the problems of subsequent generations.

The examination of the fundamental testaments of our own Revolutionary period, in the light of today's issues and interests, divulges much in these testaments that is indeed addressed to specific and particular and passing and peculiar problems of their own times; but it also divulges something about these testaments that is a continuing source of wonder to all who examine them critically. That, of course, is their curiously contemporary quality.

These were the words that moved a people toward nationhood. They were words that, at the time, were less distinguished by originality than by their suitability for the occasion on which they were employed, by their fidelity to the principles that already were widely held when they were enunciated. What has given them their universality? What has made them of more than ceremonial and commemorative consequence in these years at the end of the second century of the government they called forth?

Tom Paine's *Common Sense* was, in many ways, the most perishable of these testaments. It had the narrowest compass. It was addressed almost exclusively to the immediate issue of asserting independence. Its intellectual lens was narrowed to the sharpest focus on the weaknesses of the British

Copyright 1973 by James Russell Wiggins

government and the wisdom of separating from it. He spent his best barbs on monarchy as an institution—and what sharp barbs they were. It is easy to understand what a stir they created then.

Some of the observations in *Common Sense* can be seen now to have missed the mark. There was too much confidence and too little prescience in Paine's firm assertion that the future united strength of Britain and the colonies was a "mere presumption." He was too sure of himself when he said: "This continent would never suffer itself to be drained of inhabitants to support the British arms in either Asia, Africa, or Europe." Two great wars and many smaller ones belie that forecast. His rhetorical challenge to the advocates of reconciliation to "show a single advantage that this continent can reap by being connected with Great Britain" would get Paine a deluge of literature from the promoters of union now.

Paine's inflammatory pamphlet, for all its instant purpose, was lifted above the level of the quarrels of its own time and place, nonetheless, by a quality curiously pervasive in many of the propagandists and leaders of the American Revolution. They had a clairvoyant instinct, an extrasensory perception of the American Revolution's place in world history. "Posterity," he wrote, "are virtually involved in the contest, and will be more or less affected even to the end of time, by the proceedings now."

His attack on monarchy and hereditary succession was fashioned to destroy George III, but it had as its major premise that fundamental thesis which Jefferson was to elaborate more completely in a greater document. "Mankind," said Paine, "being originally equals in the order of creation, the equality could only be destroyed by some subsequent circumstance. . . ." It was a conception that the passage of 200 years would not destroy. It has outlasted the target at which it was aimed to become an article of faith in a surviving nation Paine could hardly have foreseen in his most optimistic moment. "Mankind, being originally equals in the order of creation" is a proposition that has had a long life on this continent.

Paine, of course, ultimately became gloomy about America. He wrote disparagingly of Jefferson and of Washington. The language of his opening paragraphs in the "Letter to George Washington" has an air of disenchantment reminiscent of many contemporary editorial writers. He wrote: "There was a time when the fame of America, moral and political, stood fair and high in the world. The lustre of her revolution extended itself to every individual; and to be a citizen of America gave a title to respect in Europe. Neither meanness nor ingratitude had been mingled in the composition of her character."

That, of course, had been all undone by what Paine described as Washington's "deceitful, if not perfidious" administration. The reproach has since been applied to many administrations.

The political longevity and current vitality of the ideas embodied in the testaments of the American Revolution, and most notably in the Declaration of Independence, no doubt derive in part from the diversity of sources upon which the Revolutionary writers drew, as well as from their reliance upon philosophies of government by no means novel or new.

If the ideas they incorporated into American papers have lived a long time, it is because they had already lived a long time. Generations of dispute had pruned away the superfluous growth and left only hardy specimens and rugged root stocks of principles already inured to criticism, scrutiny, and detraction.

That their utterances still have contemporary force is due, as well, to the circumstance that the Americans did not put all their intellectual eggs in one philosophical basket. As Bernard Bailyn has pointed out, there were "striking incongruities and contradictions" in their theories. They invoked the common law. They made appeals to precedent, and they denounced precedent. They summoned to their support "unbroken tradition evolving from time immemorial." They assumed that the "accumulation of the ages, the burden of inherited custom, contained within it a greater wisdom than any man or group of men could devise by the power of reason."[1]

They embraced with equal enthusiasm the Enlightenment rationalists, who had nothing but contempt for tradition. And they drew, as well, upon the doctrines of Puritan theologians who had not much use for the philosophes of the Enlightenment. The approach taken by the Revolutionary writers was partially a result of the natural diversity deriving from their own philosophic environment, but it may also have represented a shrewd and ingenious exertion to unite diverse elements in a common effort of revolution.

These circumstances explain in part the imperishability and current applicability of much of the Revolutionary documentary testament today—but only in part. To these accidents of history and environment, furnishing the fuel of revolution, must be added the spark of genius, to borrow a Lincoln figure of speech, the genius of Jefferson, Franklin, Madison, Adams, and other Revolutionary leaders, who dug up their ideas wherever they could find them but transmuted them by the refinements of their own intellectual metallurgy into new alloys.

The essential element of Thomas Jefferson's great Declaration of Independence really is in one incredible sentence: "We hold these truths to be self-evident, that all men are created equal, that they are endowed by their

Creator with certain unalienable Rights, that among these are Life, Liberty and the pursuit of Happiness." No one has put the matter more succinctly, or more indestructibly. It is a contemporary fashion of the New Left to dismiss the American Revolution as a retrograde movement, but no one has been able to improve upon this statement of the very purposes of popular government. Here is the distillation of the wisdom of the 17th-century liberals and their 18th-century interpreters. And it has lasted.

Many revolutionaries of the past—and many of today—invoked as their sanction for rebellion the Declaration's blunt assertion of the right of the people to abolish government destructive of these rights. Not as many, of course, advert to the admonitory note that established governments should not be changed for "light and transient" causes.

The long catalog of the "history of the present King of England," constituting so large a part of the body of the Declaration, has had its detractors, both for its doctrine linking the train of events in a conspiratorial British plot and for its specificity. No doubt the conspiratorial theory was overemphasized. The British politicians of the day, on reexamination, seem less bloody minded than muddle headed and absent minded. The enumeration of specific complaints may not be as "dated," however, as many of its critics assume. The things of which it protests are not vanished inquisitions by past arbitrary government alone. In many cases, they are trespasses not unknown in our own times, in this or in other countries.

Take the text in hand and, for the protests against the exercise of the authority of King George III, read it as a protest against the excessive use of the veto, the failure to carry out laws passed by Congress, the enforcement of immigration quotas, the proliferation of federal officials, the trespass of military upon civil power, interference with trade—and a great many more complaints about executive power in modern times.

The declaration discloses one impulse which has remained typically American to this day. Actually, the Declaration emerged in response to this impulse. I speak of the impulse to seek the approval of the world for American policy. Jefferson referred to "a decent respect for the opinions of mankind." He said, "let Facts be submitted to a candid world." It is doubtful that any government constituted among men has so frequently or fully sought to explain itself to the world. We still are doing it, and some profound change will have occurred in us when we cease doing it.

It is a mistake to dismiss this phrase as a mere explanatory footnote. It is no mere aside. It is central dogma of American beliefs, and one that revolutionary governments since have felt compelled to imitate. But although they have imitated it, few have raised their principles to the same levels of eloquence. In the decades and generations since, the appeal to the opinion of mankind may not always have been as successful, and sometimes success has not been as deserved, but the obedience to this earlier precedent has more than a mere propaganda effect.

Governments given to such an acknowledgment of the right of the rest of mankind to have an explanation of policy must adhere to sterner disciplines in the making of policy. This self-assumed burden, taken up when America was a small power indeed, has become of the utmost importance in a world so greatly influenced by the rise of American strength and power.

There were many contemporaries of Thomas Jefferson and Thomas Paine who saw their ideas of equality as a threat not only to the government then existing but to any organized government. Jonathan Boucher thought the notion that men are born equal was dangerous and fallacious: "Man differs from man in everything that can be supposed to lead to supremacy and subjection, *as one star differs from another star in glory*."[2]

Daniel Leonard said reproachfully of the patriot leaders: "They begin by reminding the people of the elevated rank they hold in the universe, as men; that all men by nature are equal; that Kings are but the ministers of the people; that their authority is delegated to them by the people for their good, and they have a right to resume it, and place it in other hands, or keep it themselves, whenever it is made use of to oppress them."[3]

In his *Pamphlets of the American Revolution,* Bernard Bailyn summarizes the doubts and fears of such conservative critics as follows: "Seeds of sedition would thus constantly be sown, and harvests of licentiousness reaped. How else could it end? What reasonable social and political order could conceivably be built and maintained where authority was questioned before it was obeyed, where social differences were considered to be incidental rather than essential to community order, and where superiority, suspect in principle, was not allowed to concentrate in the hands of a few but was scattered broadly through the populace?"[4]

There are Bouchers and Leonards still about in our day. In fact, there is a surviving, vestigial remnant of their skepticism in most of us, on occasion. A few years ago, while I was standing on the roof of the *Washington Post* building and watching a portion of this city go up in flames, the gloomy forebodings of the Bouchers and Leonards came to mind.

There have been many other moments in our turbulent history to try our faith in equality and in liberty.

Less is said about some other ideas implicit in the patriot philosophy but not so celebrated in their own literature or in current comments upon it. The kind of government envisioned in the pamphlets of the period of the American Revolution, promised in Paine, projected in Jefferson, and incorporated in the Constitution was a government that gave a great deal of latitude to public authority and to popular will—enough to allow both to err now and then on the side of restraint and now and then on the side of permissiveness.

They created a system that left room enough for government to be right and room enough for it to be wrong and did not delude themselves with the notion that they could restrict a government so that it could not make mistakes without so restricting it that it could not do anything. Because they dealt in generalizations and principles, they were providentially ambiguous—ambiguous enough to allow society room in which to move. This latitudinarianism and ambiguity has made a certain amount of tumult and tension inevitable and has forestalled, except in rare crises, the kind of open clash and direct confrontation that has doomed less flexible systems to fracture.

The pre-Revolutionary period had conditioned them to believe in conflict, controversy, debate, and disagreement, rather than to aspire to quiet public life or tranquilize human affairs. They did not put their belief in so many words, but they seem to have well understood society's psychological need for disharmony, of which Lewis Mumford has spoken so perceptively. In his book *The Culture of Cities,* he wrote:

> Reformers and renovators, whose work usually is prompted by some raucous failure in the social machinery, are tempted to oversimplify in the opposite direction: they seek a harmony too absolute, an order whose translation into actual life would stultify the very purpose it seeks to achieve. The student of utopias knows the weakness that lies in perfectionism: for that weakness has now been made manifest in the new totalitarian states, where the dreams of a Plato, a Cabet, a Bellamy have at many removes taken shape. What is lacking in such dreams is not a sense of the practical: what is lacking is a realization of the essential human need for disharmony and conflict, elements whose acceptance and resolution are indispensable to psychological growth.[5]

The American system that for nearly 200 years has withstood fluctuating fortunes of civil wars and worldwide conflicts was constructed with a little play in its moving parts. Had its bearings been fashioned with as little tolerance as some people might wish, it would have burned out long ago. This play is the terror of many timid people and is reproached by many exact people who see the vehicle of state move farther to the right than they would like and then farther to the left than they would like.

As John Motley has reminded us, "Liberal institutions, republican or constitutional governments, move in the daylight; we see their mode of

The Fundamental Testaments Today

operation, feel the jar of their wheels, and are often needlessly alarmed at their apparent tendencies."[6]

It would have pleased the patriots of the American Revolution, who generally believed with Jefferson that the "earth belongs to the living," to see each generation of Americans place its own construction upon the ringing Declaration to which they subscribed.

This generation has chosen to put more emphasis upon that pregnant word of the Declaration, "equal." Jefferson's happy modification of Locke's "property" into "the pursuit of happiness" has turned the impulses of the people and their government toward greater and greater exertions to improve mankind. Once in a while we need to be reminded that although man may be improved it is not likely that he can be perfected. The patriots were practical men who understood the difference between equality and uniformity, between improvability and perfectibility.

Jefferson, often regarded as the most hopeful and optimistic of them all, warned: "That every man shall be made virtuous, by any process whatever, is, indeed, no more to be expected, than that every tree shall be made to bear fruit, and every plant nourishment." He wisely saw a "prospect of great advancement in the happiness of the human race," but cautiously concluded that "this may proceed to an indefinite, although not to an infinite degree."[7]

The luminous phrases of our Revolutionary testaments are more likely to catch the eye in each passing generation, including our own, than the more realistic acknowledgments of the limitations on human achievement. We can be more easily roused to the arduous pursuit of happiness than we can be persuaded to accept the realization that it cannot always be achieved.

Now we are in a period of American experience in which emphasis is being put on the limitations. The reaction of the country to the efforts of the Office of Economic Opportunity is that the government attempted too much. Too optimistic an answer was given to the query: "How equal?" Were we trying to achieve "infinite" happiness instead of just indefinite progress toward human happiness? The experiment has filled some people with despair, and its failures have filled some people with delight. Perhaps we shall not know for a long time how much the shortcomings of the OEO were the result of administrative ineptitude and how much they were due to the resistance of human material to rapid change.

Perhaps we must sadly concede that a great deal of the unhappiness and injustice of the world proceeds from the inherent tragedy of the human condition. Much of this tragedy is beyond the ingenuity of governments.

Much of the misery of the human family lies beyond the reach of our social and political genius.

The current wisdom, no doubt, is that the country, in the recent past, attempted too much and tried too hard to expand that concept of equality enunciated in the Declaration of Independence. To say of a society, a government, an administration, or an era that it attempted too much and tried too hard to better the human condition is an impeachment—but it is a soft impeachment. It is, I think, fortunate that our revolutionary origins and impulses have inclined our statesmen generally to try to better the lot of mankind.

There are other critics, of course, who say that the American system never has attempted, seriously enough, to carry out the implications of the Declaration's bold assertion that men are created equal. However far equality ought to extent beyond "creation," the practical goal of a democratic society ought to be to diminish the gross disparities of power, wealth, and influence that affront any logical sense of proportionate reward for the application of industry, talent, and genius. The late R. H. Tawney once attacked $400,000-a-year salaries in a democratic society as "ungentlemanly," if not uneconomic.[8] It was Tawney who also put forth a very commonsense definition of equality, pointing out that although men "differ profoundly as individuals in capacity and character, they are equally entitled as human beings to consideration and respect, and that the well-being of a society is likely to be increased if it so plans its organization that, whether their powers are great or small, all its members may be equally enabled to make the best of such powers as they possess."[9]

The first society in the world to be officially committed to the pursuit of happiness might also do well to embrace the definition of happiness which Tawney put forth in *The Acquisitive Society*. It is a very civilized view of happiness. He said: "If a man has important work, and enough leisure and income to enable him to do it properly, he is in possession of as much happiness as is good for any of the children of Adam."[10]

Although reformers argue that it is hypocritical to continue under the noble rhetoric of the Declaration while we fall short of equality and happiness, and cynics deny that either is politically attainable, perhaps we should remember Lord Acton's conclusion that "ideals in politics are never realized, but the pursuit of them determines history."[11]

It has been our good fortune, in this symposium, to learn more about the Paris Peace Treaty of 1783. It is a neglected subject. If it had been more attended to, there never would have grown up in this country the myth that the United States always wins its wars and loses its negotiations.

The Fundamental Testaments Today

The performance of Franklin, Adams, and Jay has not been equaled in diplomatic history—at least not until the performance of Henry Kissinger in negotiating another treaty of Paris in 1973.

The situations, of course, were not identical. But the spirits of the earlier negotiators, if they hovered over the conference tables, must have been intrigued by some similarities. Here again was a great power attempting to negotiate the independence of a small and dependent ally. The United States of 1783 was caught up in the great power struggles of France, Spain, and England, and the wily Americans, by the most adroit diplomacy, succeeded in extricating from the conflicts of the great powers the essential conditions of American independence.

The South Vietnamese were also caught up in worldwide power struggles, and managed to extract at least a chance of independence. The negotiations were preceded by similar byplay: France, in 1780, urging the Americans to formulate their peace terms and suggesting a ceasefire, prodding them to concessions, pushing them toward Americanization of the war, as the mounting expenses of the struggle plagued the French regime; the Americans urging the South Vietnamese to concessions, pressing them to a ceasefire, prodding them to the Vietnamization of the war. The parallel, on one point at least, is beyond dispute. The myth that we always lose at the conference table what we have won on the battlefield has been belied, at least once, in Paris.

The contrast between the America of 1783 and the America of 1973 is so great as to raise anew the question posed here today. Think of that small 18th-century country, 3 million people, occupying a narrow strip along the Atlantic seaboard, without any effective governmental institutions, with no military force of consequence, with an untried theory of rule, with inexperienced leaders. And think of the 20th-century country, its 200 million people spanning a continent, its institutions of government the most effective and efficient in the world, its military power unsurpassed, its principles of government vindicated by two centuries of success, its leaders long experienced in government.

What do the testaments of that small, embryonic state have to say to the great nation it has become?

Oddly enough, they have more to say than ever before, because they are filled with wisdom that counsels restraint in the exercise of great power—restraint in the application of that power abroad, restraint in the imposition of that power on citizens at home. And the greater the nation becomes, the greater the country becomes, and the more powerful its government becomes, the more it needs that wisdom.

These ancient testaments have much to say, in addition, because the government which emerged from them, for all its power and might, has its elements of fragility, inherent in its principles. Abraham Lincoln said it was a government "conceived in Liberty, and dedicated to the proposition that all men are created equal." And he said the Civil War was a test of whether a government so constituted could long endure. The end of that war was not the end of the test. We still stand, in the words of Thornton Wilder, "moment by moment, on the razor edge of danger." This government is prey, as governments under no other systems are, to the fluctuating whims, passions, and prejudices of transient majorities. There was comfort in the past in the thought that momentary errors of a majority might be subsequently corrected, and the Ship of State, temporarily adrift, once more put on a right course. In the present state of the world, this no longer is so sure a consolation. The margin for error diminishes in a thermonuclear world. Perhaps we have forever lost the luxury of a little electoral mistake now and then.

If we are to survive error of this kind, we must take counsel of one of the homely admonitions of the Revolutionary period, the admonition that the choice of the rebelling colonies was between hanging together and hanging separately. A lively sense of self-preservation, sharpened by that injunction, induced the citizens of 13 separate colonies, of countless diverse and quarreling factions, to sink their differences in a common cause. We may have to sink our differences, or subdue the vigor with which we contend over them, if the 18th-century testaments by which we live are to remain living documents.

If we succeed in this endeavor, we may be able to say again, as Benjamin Rush said in 1787, "The American War is over; but this is far from being the case with the American Revolution. On the contrary, nothing but the first act of the great drama is closed."

Notes

[1] Bernard Bailyn, *The Ideological Origins of the American Revolution* (Cambridge: Belknap Press of Harvard University Press, 1967), p. 33.

[2] Quoted in Bernard Bailyn, ed., *Pamphlets of the American Revolution, 1750–1776*, vol. 1, 1750–1765 (Cambridge: Belknap Press of Harvard University Press, 1965), p. 200.

[3] Daniel Leonard, *Massachusettensis* (Boston: 1775), Letter III, December 26, 1774, p. 18.

[4] Bailyn, *Pamphlets*, 1:202.

[5] Lewis Mumford, *The Culture of Cities* (New York: Harcourt, Brace and Co., 1938), p. 485.

[6] John Lothrop Motley, *The Rise of the Dutch Republic*, 3 vols. (London: John Murray, 1903–4), 2:335.

[7] Thomas Jefferson to C. C. Blatchly, October 21, 1822, in *The Writings of Thomas Jefferson*, Monticello Edition, Andrew A. Lipscomb, editor-in-chief, vol. 15 (Washington: Issued under the auspices of the Thomas Jefferson Memorial Association of the United States, 1904), pp. 399–400.

[8] R. H. Tawney, *The Acquisitive Society* (New York: Harcourt, Brace and Co., 1920), p. 178.

[9] R. H. Tawney, *Equality* (London: G. Allen & Unwin, Ltd., 1931), p. 47.

[10] Tawney, *Acquisitive Society*, p. 179.

[11] John E. E. D. Acton, Baron, *Lord Acton and his Circle*, ed. Abbot Gasquet (London: G. Allen, 1906), p. 132.

JAMES RUSSELL WIGGINS began his career in journalism in 1922 as a reporter for the *Rock County Star*, Luverne, Minn. He became editor and publisher of the *Luverne Star* in 1925 and in 1930 joined the staff of the *Dispatch-Pioneer Press* in St. Paul, Minn., as an editorial writer. He became the newspaper's Washington correspondent in 1933 and its managing editor in 1938.

Mr. Wiggins joined the U.S. Army Air Corps in 1942 and served in the Mediterranean theater as an air combat intelligence specialist. He was discharged from the Air Corps with the rank of major and returned to St. Paul to become editor of the *Dispatch-Pioneer Press*. He accepted an appointment as assistant to the publisher of the *New York Times* in 1946.

Mr. Wiggins' association with the *Washington Post* began in 1947, when he was named managing editor of that newspaper. He became, in addition, vice president of the *Post* in 1953, and in 1955, after the merger of the *Post* and the *Times-Herald*, he was named vice president and executive editor. In 1960 he was designated editor and executive vice president, a position which he held until 1968, when he was appointed Permanent Representative of the United States to the United Nations, with the rank of ambassador extraordinary and plenipotentiary.

Mr. Wiggins has received honorary degrees from Colby College, the University of Maine, and Bates College and is the author of *Freedom or Secrecy*, published in 1956. He is a past president of the American Society of Newspaper Editors and is currently president of the American Antiquarian Society. Since his resignation as ambassador to the U.N. in 1969 he has been editor and publisher of the *Ellsworth American*, Ellsworth, Maine.

Library of Congress Publications for the Bicentennial of the American Revolution

The American Revolution: A Selected Reading List. 1968. 38 p. 50 cents. For sale by the Superintendent of Documents, U.S. Government Printing Office, Washington, D.C. 20402.

The Boston Massacre, 1770, engraved by Paul Revere. Facsim. $2.00. For sale by the Information Office, Library of Congress, Washington, D.C. 20540.

Creating Independence, 1763–1789: Background Reading for Young People. A Selected Annotated Bibliography. 1972. 62 p. 75 cents. For sale by the Superintendent of Documents, U.S. Government Printing Office, Washington, D.C. 20402.

The Development of a Revolutionary Mentality. Papers presented at the first Library of Congress Symposium on the American Revolution. 1972. 158 p. $3.50. For sale by the Information Office, Library of Congress, Washington, D.C. 20540.

English Defenders of American Freedoms 1774–1778: Six Pamphlets Attacking British Policy. 1972. 231 p. $2.75. For sale by the Superintendent of Documents, U.S. Government Printing Office, Washington, D.C. 20402.

Periodical Literature on the American Revolution: Historical Research and Changing Interpretations, 1895–1970. 1971. 93 p. $1. For sale by the Superintendent of Documents, U.S. Government Printing Office, Washington, D.C. 20402.

Two Rebuses from the American Revolution. Facsim. $2.50. For sale by the Information Office, Library of Congress, Washington, D.C. 20540.